I0123381

VOLUNTEERS

WHY YOU NEVER HAVE ENOUGH

BY BRIAN ROBEY

Copyright © 2024

Brian Robey

All rights reserved.

:

Edited by Shauna Greco

Real Volunteer Stories obtained by permission

All surveys done with voluntary participation through the Facebook Groups: *Children's Pastors Only* and *Youth Ministry Collective.*

To Toni,

my greatest volunteer, champion, and love of my life.

To Mitch Harrison,

who helped me believe that what I had was enough.

CONTENTS

6

INTRODUCTION

In all my years of ministry, there has been one recurring issue in every church, no matter the size. This issue affects nearly every ministry in every area of the country, rich churches and poor churches, rural churches and urban churches; it is the issue of having enough volunteers. While plenty of church ministries have their struggles with finding an adequate number of volunteers every week, I want to focus specifically on kids and youth ministry volunteers because it is the greatest area of need across the board for leaders of kids and youth ministries. To say we are desperate for volunteers in family ministries would not be overstating the severity of the need, and to say that those in charge of these ministries often feel overwhelmed and helpless would be an understatement.

Thanks to a global pandemic, churches had to quickly shift how we ministered. And now, after a few years of returning to "normal," I have come to realize that things will never quite be the same for our leaders or our kids. Maybe we aren't wearing masks anymore, maybe we aren't bathing in hand sanitizer like we were when the OMICRON variant spiked in 2021, but we won't ever return to how things were in 2019.

My story may be similar to yours…

At the start of the pandemic, I was a Children's Pastor in a conservative part of Georgia. Going into 2020, I had grand plans for what our kids were going to do, including our first Pre-Teen Retreat, a new immersive story family-style VBS, and equipping leaders to be live storytellers and worship leaders. And all of it was canceled. I was sidelined and relegated to doing nothing more than making lesson videos every week to post for kids in hopes that they would be willing to sit in front of their screens for an additional 15 minutes.

It was a rough 4 months.

In May, our church was one of the first to open up, and we gradually started adding children's ministry classes back in June and July. By August, we had all our rooms open again, but with only about half our children's ministry volunteers feeling comfortable returning. In September, word started getting out that our church had opened our children's ministry, and we started getting families from some of the larger churches that were still holding virtual services. As a result, our children's ministry was back to pre-COVID numbers by the end of 2020, but with less than half the volunteers we had before. Historically, our ratios of volunteers to kids were never ideal, but now I was one call-out away from a Lord of the Flies scenario every Sunday.

I knew other Children's and Youth pastors were also feeling like they did not have enough volunteers. After all, this was not a new problem, but COVID put more strain on what was already an area of great struggle for leaders. I decided to poll other family ministry leaders to see where they were at.

Giving four options to the Children's Pastors Only Facebook group, I received close to 400 responses—a vast number of which echoed my suspicions that our ministries were critically understaffed. Having enough volunteers was a universal issue for children's ministry leaders across the country and even around the world. If this was the case, then the issue had to run deeper than just the hesitant return to serving after the pandemic. Recruiting volunteers had always been a challenge, even before the pandemic.

And if that was the case, then there was a larger problem, and it was affecting churches everywhere.

Churches large and small are desperate for volunteers, and I believe that desperation stems directly from trying to do ministry in a way that exceeds God's provision for our ministries. I think children's ministries and youth ministries got to this place because we have focused heavily on vision and ignored the stark realities of what God has given us to work with.

This is where I believe the book you're about to read can really help your ministry—not just with some handy recruiting tools or a better system for onboarding new volunteers—but by learning to use the leaders, space, and resources God has given you effectively. While I think there are tools that can benefit youth ministries as well as children's ministries in the pages to follow, I am writing this from years of experience as a children's Pastor, and you may notice a tendency toward children's ministry examples.

In addition to changing how you look at your resources, I also think it is important to help you and your leaders guard against burnout so that you do not have to replace the leaders who were just recruited. As the leader of the ministry, I want you to find ways to ensure the responsibilities of your role will not drain you from your purpose.

My prayer for you, as you read this book, is that God will help you operate your ministry from a place of contentment and that contentment will eventually lead to abundance, freeing you up to search out the methods and means God wants you to utilize in sharing the Gospel of Jesus Christ with kids and families in your church. I pray that this book helps lift the burden you feel as you emerge from the chaos and uncertainty of a global pandemic and gives you peace and confidence to lead your ministry in a healthy, God-honoring way.

CHAPTER ONE

HOW DID WE GET HERE?

There is one phrase I hear from church leaders more than any other; it's the phrase, "I need more volunteers." Having spent time on staff in churches both large and small, I often found myself thinking the same things:

If only we had 5 more leaders, then we could do _____.

One of my volunteers just quit; how am I going to keep that small group going?

The worship team has 25 people who want to sing; I'd settle for 2 who want to work with toddlers?

Super-big-multi-site-church down the street has a full live band to lead worship for youth. How great would it be if we had something like that?

The truth is that leaders have been spoon-fed a model for doing ministry—especially children's and youth ministry—that ignores a fundamental truth about church resources. The largest churches and their models for ministry are examples for the rest of us to admire and imitate. As a result, children's ministry has become an arms race to build Disneyland-caliber kids' areas complete with playgrounds and light shows. Youth groups spend tens or even hundreds of thousands of dollars building impressive youth spaces to keep students from going somewhere else. The example of a successful ministry showcased for all to see is always large scale, big budget, and its flaws airbrushed.

No matter how many conferences I go to, I still have not heard a pastor from a church with 200 members being invited to speak. I don't see a kids' ministry of 25 featured in a ministry publication. It's almost as if the ministry happening in small churches is irrelevant or inconsequential, even though a vast majority of churches around the world are "small." A Hartford Institute for Religion Research study concluded that less than 0.5% of churches in America have an attendance of over 1800 members. Think about that…half of one percent of all churches are big. So, if 95.5% of churches do not have the resources, manpower, or facilities that the largest churches have, then why are these large churches dictating every ministry model and trend? It's no wonder we are burning out leaders when we expect them to imitate a ministry model that has more staff, more funding, and a larger pool of potential volunteers to make it run.

A pastor with 75 congregants comes away feeling like a failure because her church can't do what the bigger churches are doing, but is that actually true? Is the ministry in a smaller church somehow less important than the ministry in a large church? That's definitely not how God sees it since small churches make up a far bigger portion of active churches.

So how does this big church versus small church debate relate to volunteers, you might ask?

After seminary, I landed a position in one of the largest churches on the West Coast. Coming from my previous part-time position at a church of 200, this felt like going from an AA minor league team to the majors. The church averaged 10,000 members each weekend across its 4 campuses. I worked at the mother church location where we had around 1,000 kids between the ages of 0-11 each weekend in one of 5 services. Every book I had read, and formula I had studied led me to believe this would be a dream job. Working at an influential kids' ministry where other churches regularly came to us to see what we were doing and how they could emulate that approach was very exciting. I was one of 3 children's ministry directors for our campus, and together, we oversaw about 300 kids' ministry leaders. This church had a bigger budget for VBS than my last church's total annual budget.

But after a few months, I heard a phrase I thought I would never hear in a ministry this size; "Once we get about 20 more volunteers, we can do that." Wait, what? We already had 300 volunteers! That's a church in itself! What can we do with 320 volunteers that we can't do with 300? What I realized at that moment was that even at the largest churches, there was no ceiling on the number of volunteers an organization believes it needs. Pastors and leaders in almost every ministry believe they are short of volunteers. In every children's ministry, in every church size, and in every corner of the country, we are all begging and pleading for more help. As a result, pastors, directors, coordinators, and leaders are burning out in record numbers because they feel like they are being asked to bring vision and leadership to a ministry without adequate help and support.

WHICH CHOICE BEST DESCRIBES YOUR CHILDREN'S MINISTRY RIGHT

205 We need at least 10 more volunteers for our ministry to run smoothly

143 If we had 5 more volunteers we'd be in great shape

67 We have enough volunteers

1 Help! I'm drowning in volunteers!

Needless to say, a vast majority of children's ministry leaders are desperate for more volunteers. Youth ministry, while not quite as lop-sided, is also short-staffed with adult leaders.

The pandemic did not do us any favors with our volunteer pool either. I lost nearly half my children's ministry leaders when our church reopened in June 2020. So, if every church seems to be struggling with this issue, something is out of balance. Church leaders must be doing something wrong if, across denominations, church sizes, and demographics, established and young church plants alike are all feeling like the harvest is plentiful, but the workers are few. I'm sure there are plenty of Children's Pastors with far more experience than myself who could offer great insights, but no one else seems to want to address the elephant in the room or clean up after it.

WHICH CHOICE BEST DESCRIBES YOUR YOUTH MINISTRY RIGHT NOW?

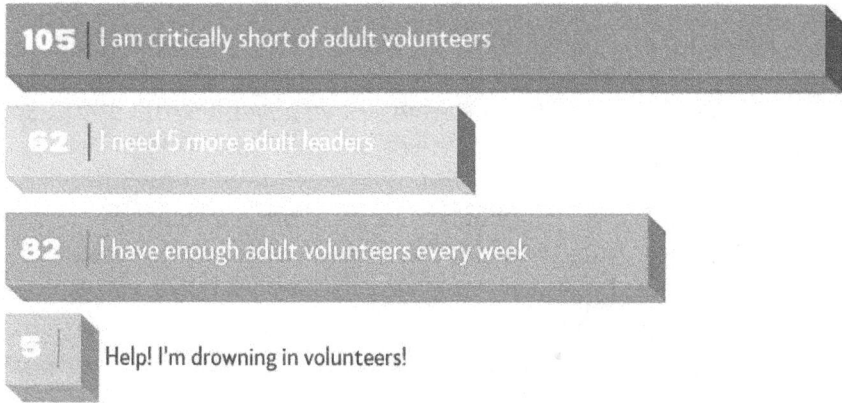

105 I am critically short of adult volunteers

62 I need 5 more adult leaders

82 I have enough adult volunteers every week

5 Help! I'm drowning in volunteers!

Was it always this way? Should we be blaming a culture that is less and less interested in serving? Do we need to pressure church leadership to make serving mandatory? The truth of the matter is that churches are simply trying to make a square peg (the vision for your ministry as influenced by larger churches and organizations) fit in a round hole (what your church has to work with). We are making our plans and then taking them to God and asking him to bless them, never taking the time to meditate on why we want growth or why we need to do what we've set out to do. We are victims of a veiled greed we didn't even realize was present in our ministry: being discontent with the resources, facilities, and leaders God has given us and wishing we had more.

One summer in college, I took an unpaid internship with a church in Las Vegas in their worship department. This was a very creative church that was finding plenty of innovative ways to share the gospel. It was my first exposure to vocational ministry, other than what I had experienced being a pastor's kid. I was paid in the form of a weekly lunch meeting with the Pastor of the Artist Community. He would spend an hour or two pouring out the philosophy of ministry and some extremely important inside information about ministry leadership. The most formative thing I took away from that summer was a phrase that eventually became my philosophy for ministry:

God gives you exactly what you need to do the ministry. He wants you to do.

It's so simple and obvious…but I have never heard it anywhere else.

When Jesus is teaching his disciples to pray, he teaches them to ask God to give us daily bread. I'm sure if you've been in children's ministry for any length of time, you've even taught kids in your ministry this concept of God providing for the needs of that particular day. Jesus tells us not to pray for a month's worth of provisions. We shouldn't pray for $1,000,000 to cover all expenses for the next 15 years. That's not daily bread. Jesus knew that once we had a stockpile of resources, we would stop needing God and would rely on ourselves to protect or enrich the stockpile. Daily bread is a daily trust that here and now, God can meet our immediate needs, and the future needs need not be worried about. But we don't think about ministry strategies like this. We have been taught that we have to plan for growth, and we need to focus on what our ministry will need next year, the next 5 or 10 years.

How many leaders, after having led their kids or youth ministries during the COVID shutdown, discovered how quickly their 1 year or 5-year plans were tossed in the wastebasket? If I took away one big lesson from the pandemic, it's that I have to be nimble and responsive to the conditions that families are facing. Every Pastor was scrambling to figure out how to adjust for conditions they had never seen or planned for. It was unprecedented because, all of a sudden, the size of your church wasn't important. The bells and whistles that so many churches were proud of and others were envious of were instantly irrelevant. We began to see that smaller congregations could adapt faster, while larger churches were bogged down in an endless series of Zoom meetings trying to figure out what the church would look like if it didn't involve a large crowd in their building.

Instead of diving into a social media gumbo of ideas that this church or that church was trying, I instead prayed this prayer:

God, I know you have given me exactly what I need to do the ministry you want me to do during this pandemic. Show me what that looks like. Help me not to get caught up in chasing gimmicks or trends, but let me see the ministry as you want it to be.

For the first time in 50 years, children's and youth ministries had the opportunity to press the reset button. We could now do something completely new and tear down some of the idols we had built up for ourselves that focused more on numbers or facilities. During the shutdown, there was only the leader's heart for their people and an unscripted story on how they would share Jesus now that none of these idols were in the way. The mainstream thinking in ministry was turned on its head because now, a children's director with 20 kids in their ministry had an advantage over the children's director with 500 kids.

Having kids of my own, I quickly came to realize the challenges facing families during the pandemic. Everyone was thrust in front of a screen. In-person contact became impossible. Isolation became an unwelcome houseguest. So, instead of trying to do our usual programming through some kind of video chat, I thought about what the kids in my ministry really needed. They didn't need another screen to stare at. They really needed to know they weren't forgotten and they were important. So, I decided to write every kid in my ministry a card asking them how I could pray for them and mail it to them. I set up 1 on 1 virtual hangout where kids showed me what they were up to while they were stuck at home. I now had time to just listen to kids one on one, even if it looked a little different. My goal was to help them feel known and cared for in some small way—to know that they mattered. Imagine that—a pastor caring for the needs of the flock. What a revolutionary idea! I felt like all the extra stuff that had been tied to "doing ministry" had suddenly been cut off. But that's when I started getting pushback from church leadership, who were worried the kids' ministry wasn't "doing enough."

GOD GIVES YOU EXACTLY WHAT YOU NEED TO DO THE MINISTRY HE WANTS YOU TO DO

In the Star Wars movie The Last Jedi, there's a fitting scene where Kylo Ren and Rey are in the throne room of Supreme Leader Snoke. Kylo ends up killing Snoke, and an epic fight with his guards ensues. Once Kylo and Rey take out all of the guards, Rey races to a control panel to try to stop the attack against her friends. But Kylo points out that this is the moment she can let it all burn down: the First Order, the Resistance, the Jedi, the Sith. Right now, she can join him and start something new without the burden of previous constructs requiring her to be on one side or another. They can create a new door to walk through where they don't have to fight with one another. But Rey refuses to join Kylo in this new possibility. To that decision, Kylo yells back, "You're still holding on!" He is frustrated by her stubborn desire to keep things the same, thereby continuing the fight.

The sad truth is it's much harder to burn things down than we make it out to be. I'd be willing to bet for all those sermons we heard during the shutdown about COVID being a wake-up call for churches and how we needed to take this opportunity to do ministry differently, churches ran—no, sprinted—back to what was comfortable once things reopened. If you attended a service now, it would be almost identical to a service from 2019, and the same would be true of youth and kid's ministries.

We like what's known, what works, and what is quantifiable. And it didn't take long for pastors and leaders to settle back into the familiar groove of a ministry model that was broken and inherently unsustainable, holding on to something we know that has proven to frustrate, dishearten, and burn out countless leaders for decades.

Are you frustrated with the grind of finding volunteers, losing volunteers, and finding more volunteers? Do you feel like you're spinning your wheels because you simply don't have the time or bandwidth to recruit on top of all your other ministry responsibilities?

If you answered yes to these questions, then you're ready to try a new way of utilizing volunteers. It will be different. There will be pushback. You will need to help your church leadership understand what you're doing differently. That challenge is probably enormous enough for most leaders to throw this book in the trash and say forget it.

You have to embrace the truth—that God has given you the exact volunteers, families, resources, and space to do the ministry he wants you to do. Instead of trying to keep failing at making that square peg fit in the round hole, make a new round peg that fits.

There are a few big things to this process that we will look at in this book. First, we will focus on how to identify what God has given you and look at new ways to use it.

Second, we will take inventory of your plans for the ministry and spend some time getting to the root of why you or your church wants those plans in the first place. Most importantly, we will focus on how to view the volunteers God wants in your ministry and how to keep them fulfilled as they co-labor with you in your ministry.

Retention is also a huge part of this shift. Learning how to steward what God has given you by not burning out or frustrating those who lead with you will go a long way. The most crucial idea is to find the right model for your ministry to flourish within the constraints of your specific church.

Once I stopped trying to get God on board with my ambitious 5-year plan for my ministry and rethink how I was utilizing what God had entrusted me with, God started entrusting me with more. It seems incredibly counter-intuitive, but once I stopped trying to recruit volunteers just to satisfy a quota or get a new program off the ground, God just led new volunteers through my office door. It was almost like God's way was easier and more fruitful than my own way of doing ministry—crazy, right?

CHAPTER TWO

DESPERATE TIMES & DESPERATE MEASURES

It's crazy to think that Children's Ministry and Youth Ministry as we know them are barely a hundred years old. Programmatic, age-specific ministry is still relatively in its infancy compared to liturgical worship services.

Many churches developed age-specific catechisms that date back hundreds of years to instruct children on theology or church doctrine—and many still do today. John Calvin had an organized plan for the discipleship of children in 1537.[1] As Calvin continued to develop this catechism in the following years, he wrote that this Christian education focused on youngsters was meant as a *compliment* to church services—not as a *competitor*.

A need was seen for specialized teaching of the Bible at an age-appropriate level, and church leaders got behind the initiative with resources and facilities. For a number of years, the Sunday School Hour was the main place for children to encounter specialized

---

[1] Jones, Timothy Family Ministry: *When and Where Did Weekly Children's Classes Begin in Churches Part 1, 2017.*

Biblical education, with most churches still including children in their primary worship services.

Today, hundreds of books have been devoted to the undertaking of ministry to kids and middle/high school students. There are over 20 children's and youth ministry curriculum companies for English-speaking American churches, in addition to church denominations writing lessons for their own churches.

I truly believe each of these companies have an earnest desire to see kids come to know Jesus and learn the Bible. I believe children's ministry and youth ministry came out of the same pure, God-given desire to help kids know God at their level. But let me ask you a real question that requires you to do some soul searching and be brutally honest: *is the ministry you provide to kids or teens complementing or competing with your worship services?*

In 1894, a Sunday school teacher names D.T. Miles, who was also a public school teacher, started a 4-week long summer program devoted to thoroughly teaching the Bible to children. This summer Bible teaching model grew among the Baptist churches in the Midwest, eventually becoming what we now call Vacation Bible School by the middle of the 1920s. This was the cutting edge of ministry to kids, and it reaped huge dividends for the kids that benefited from this ground-breaking, age-specific Christian education. So, when did we switch from kid's ministry being a complement of Sunday services to being a competitor? It's hard to point to a certain church or certain year. My personal theory has more to do with the rise of Nickelodeon and the kid's cartoons of the early 1980s. While there had always been entertainment for kids, advertising firms started targeting the huge untapped market of kids and teens. Advertisers began aggressively wooing these age groups using multiple advertising strategies. More more cable networks popped up, catering exclusively to child and teenage markets. These networks could be viewed not just on Saturday morning or after school but as an alternative to the prime-time network shows that were made with an adult audience in mind. Kids in the 1980s now had an alternative to programming that was made for their parents, and churches began to notice.

When you tailored the Gospel to engage with kids the same way Nickelodeon, MTV or Disney did, you could actually get—and keep—kid's attention. The reality was, kids were being influenced by these media networks and the advertising that supported them, and churches were going to have to up their game if they didn't want kids to check out at church. The big advantage for churches was that, unlike Disneyland, where families may come once in a lifetime or at most once a year, families came to their churches on a regular basis. This is when you started to see churches invest heavily in the theming of their kids and youth areas as well as specialized curriculum that mirrored the experience kids would have watching Nickelodeon or Disney Channel.

Once a few churches started theming out their facilities, it became a sort of arms race to have an attractive, creatively decorated space tied to fun, memorable lessons and activities. But this left smaller churches—or at least churches with smaller budgets— at a disadvantage. While their education programs may have been superb, and their leaders may have been great at connecting with kids, families shopping around for a new church would be comparing the facilities of larger, wealthier churches to the ordinary facilities of smaller churches.

The idea of church shopping also began to be more widely accepted. Christian families were not going to a church with the mindset that they were joining a community in which they were expected to be an active participant, but rather, they were looking for what the church had to offer them. Churches were being compared to one another like gyms or country clubs and these churches were left vying for the attendance of families in the area. It didn't take long for smaller churches to feel the need to make investments in theming and curriculum to be considered a "desirable" church for a young family—the lifeblood of healthy churches.

You might be thinking, "Thanks for the history lesson, but what does this have to do with volunteers?"

We have put so much time, energy, and resources into the environments our kids and teens experience in church because we have bought into the idea that a well-designed environment communicates its importance. In doing so, we have missed the true resource that our churches can leverage with this generation: personal relationships with caring adults. Our ministry workers are the true jewel of any youth or children's ministry because they can actually care about an individual and make a life-changing investment in a child or student. Yet, we spend so little of our time, resources and focus on our volunteers. Is it any wonder we are always short on help?

We all know that if our church building were to burn to the ground on Monday, it would be our volunteers who would keep our ministry moving. The building, the bells and whistles-none of that really makes a lasting impact on anyone in your ministry. What's hip and relevant today will be outdated and cringe-worthy tomorrow, but someone who actually cares about what's happening in your life will never get old.

When the disciples stood in the temple courts in awe of the imposing architecture, it was Jesus who replied that soon, not one stone would be left standing on another. No matter how beautiful the building is, it is a temporary, lifeless thing. If we get caught up in an arms race of best decorated kid's area or post-worthy youth spaces, we can easily neglect the value of an unpaid volunteer who sacrifices their time not out of obligation or penalty but truly to influence and impact those who need to know Jesus in a deeper way. This is what Jesus wanted when he commanded us to make disciples—a relationship that fosters faith—not a building or a program that everyone fawns over.

Time and time again, we are fed the opposite narrative. Ministry leaders are continually bombarded with messages from "successful" churches sharing proven strategies and methods for reaching youngsters, and it never seems to be simply about finding the right people to invest in them. There's always a study or a DVD or a subscription tacked on to the promise of growing your ministry or being relevant. There's not a lot of money in helping people recruit volunteers. It's not something you can hire a design firm to help, with and it can't really be made into an 8-week small group series.

WHAT DOES YOUR CHILDREN'S MINISTRY NEED MOST?

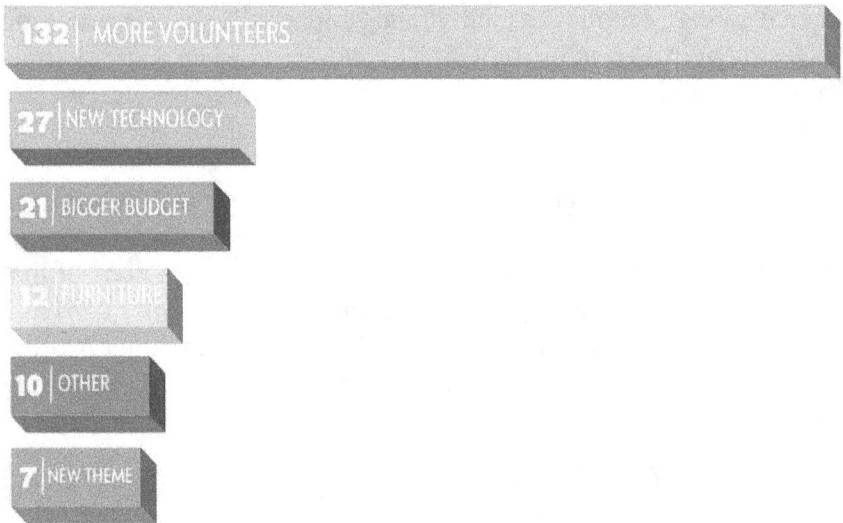

132 MORE VOLUNTEERS

27 NEW TECHNOLOGY

21 BIGGER BUDGET

12 FURNITURE

10 OTHER

7 NEW THEME

The greatest irony is that when you ask a Children's Pastor what they need most, volunteers seem to *almost always* be more pressing than a new space or new equipment. I surveyed over 200 children's pastors, asking them what their ministry needed most. I listed all the things that I've heard various pastors lament about having a bigger budget, new technology like an A/V system or TVs, kid-appropriate classroom furniture, and even a new theme for their kids' space. But with all of these needs, the heavy favorite was "MORE VOLUNTEERS" by a 5 to 1 ratio. Pastors would rather have more volunteers than more money to work with. They would rather have more volunteers than a state-of-the-art kid's space.

We can manage with lean budgets, old tables, broken crayons and even multi-use rooms that we can't decorate. What we consistently need are co-laborers to help us in our ministry. While we're led to believe that flashy and expensive investments attract new families, what makes those families *stay* at your church are the people. It is painfully evident that what our youth and children's ministries need most are people. However, when we look at the industries that have sprung up to support family ministries, very few have anything to do with recruiting, keeping, or developing volunteers. We have numerous choices for curriculum, countless options for companies that construct playgrounds or design wonderlands to amaze kids in our building. We have countless books on how to run an effective youth ministry, kid's ministry, and family ministry. We even have consultants who can come into your church and diagnose potential issues.

THE BEST RESOURCE THAT OUR CHURCHES CAN LEVERAGE WITH THIS GENERATION IS PERSONAL RELATIONSHIPS.

What churches seem to be lacking is assistance in finding the *right* volunteers. Our methods for trying to recruit volunteers yield few takers, if they work at all, and we put our faith in well-placed ads in the bulletin or announcements from the stage/pulpit to fill the greatest need in our ministry. The trouble is that these strategies create almost as many problems as they solve.

Your ministry comes off as desperate and disorganized to those who hear or see you beg for help. It also makes serving with kids or youth is undesirable or difficult.

It's akin to being desperate to find love on dating websites. The first thing you do is create a profile to attract a future mate. In trying to appeal to as many potential suitors as possible, your list of desirable traits in a potential mate becomes broad and vague, raising red flags for others who see your profile. In hopes of not scaring anyone off, you don't disclose much personal information, making others wonder if you are actually real. Your profile reeks of desperation while being impersonal at the same time, and instead of getting the desired result—a large pool from which to choose—your choices are few.

The volunteer recruitment process can be the same way. If you try to appeal to everyone in your church, you will end up recruiting people who have no passion for kids. If you pressure people into serving in your ministry, they will usually bolt at the first opportunity. If you don't have detailed descriptions of the positions in your ministry, you may spend time and energy trying to make the wrong people fit in a role that was never a good fit for them.

I don't know anyone who has made a great decision when they are in a desperate position. Desperation causes us to compromise in areas that can expose our ministries up to dangers and huge headaches.

So, the first thing we have to do when looking for leaders is to realize we are not desperate. We have to remember that we are not ultimately in charge of our ministry…God is. With God in charge, it's important to remember the saying I learned as an intern: God gives you exactly what you need to do the ministry he wants you to do.

Real Life Volunteer Stories

"I have a volunteer we'll call Lisa. Lisa has only been a volunteer for a year or so. She has two young children (ages 5 and 2) and volunteers as a teacher for our Children's Church time which is K-5. She recently asked me if we could split that group in half to try to deal with some behavior issues. She felt like smaller groups might be helpful. I told her it had been a longtime goal of mine, but I had never had the manpower to make it happen. Every time we got a new volunteer, someone else seemed to step down. Her response was one of the best things I've ever experienced. She said "How many people do you need?" I told her 4 would be ideal, but I could make it work with 3.

Within 24 hours, she had 4 new volunteers for me! She was able to appeal to them in a way I couldn't. She told them how I print and prepare everything to try to make things easy for them. She asked her family members and coworkers and friends who attend our church. I truly believe those new volunteers might have turned me down, but because of her boldness, we are able to do something desperately needed in our ministry. I am so, so grateful for her!"

Chelsea Powell

Glendale Christian Church

Glendale, Kentucky

CHAPTER THREE

OPERATING IN THE BLACK

If you are in ministry—whether full time, part time or volunteer—it's important to be guided by a personal philosophy of ministry. During my time in seminary, we dedicated considerable effort to honing our personal philosophies of ministry. These are not statements of faith or a list of essential doctrines. A philosophy of ministry is the guiding principle by which you approach being a minister of the Gospel. Years before, I had a mentor share an amazing philosophy of ministry that I carried into my ministry career.

It was a scorching Las Vegas summer in 2002. I was serving as an intern at Canyon Ridge Christian Church, being paid in experience and the occasional lunch with Mitch Harrison, the Pastor of Artist Community there at that time.

I always took a notebook to our lunch meetings as he would drop pearls of wisdom. I was a college student who had mostly seen ministry through the lens of being a pastor's kid. This internship was so formative to learn about how to *do* ministry and how to think about ministry. Among the many great insights Mitch shared with me, the most impactful was this:

God gives you exactly what you need to do the ministry he wants you do.

This statement has some huge ramifications, mostly because it challenges us to let go of preconceived notions about church and instead, trust that God is in control. It can be overwhelming to enter ministry and see all the short-comings. Focusing on limitations or what we may lead us to hastily assemble a version of the ministry we think we need, robbing ourselves of the peace God invites us to experience.

Jesus articulates this concept in Matthew 6 during his sermon on the mount. Reading it in the Message translation helps me hear what Jesus is saying in a new way, as I've read these verses hundreds of time before.

"If you decide for God, living a life of God-worship, it follows that you don't fuss about what's on the table at mealtimes or whether the clothes in your closet are in fashion. There is far more to your life than the food you put in your stomach, more to your outer appearance than the clothes you hang on your body. Look at the birds, free and unfettered, not tied down to a job description, careless in the care of God. And you count far more to him than birds.

27–29 "Has anyone by fussing in front of the mirror ever gotten taller by so much as an inch? All this time and money wasted on fashion—do you think it makes that much difference? Instead of looking at the fashions, walk out into the fields and look at the wildflowers. They never primp or shop, but have you ever seen color and design quite like it? The ten best-dressed men and women in the country look shabby alongside them.

30–33 "If God gives such attention to the appearance of wildflowers—most of which are never even seen—don't you think he'll attend to you, take pride in you, do his best for you? What I'm trying to do here is to get you to relax, to not be so preoccupied with getting, so you can respond to God's giving. People who don't know God and the way he works fuss over these things, but you know both

God and how he works. Steep your life in God-reality, God-initiative, God-provisions. Don't worry about missing out. You'll find all your everyday human concerns will be met.

Matthew 6:25-33 The Message Translation[2]

What I'm trying to do here is to get you to relax, to not be so preoccupied with getting, so you can respond to God's giving.

Wow!

When you read it like that, it's evident that Jesus encourages us not to stress out over our possessions but to trust in God's provision. We have everything God wants us to have and everything God knows we need, so why are we freaking out?

All of us give these verses in Matthew lip service—we may even teach others this sermon, telling them not to worry. However, the rubber meets the road on Sunday morning. It's 10 minutes before service and three of my volunteers are MIA. Can I relax in God's provision in that moment or am I sweating and scrambling to find substitutes? It can be so hard to juxtapose these two conflicting views: one, that God has everything under control, and the other, that I have a room full of kindergarteners who won't have a leader unless I act....right now.

One of the most important words in this philosophy is EXACTLY. God doesn't provide an outdated version of what you need. God doesn't give you a fixer-upper that will eventually meet your need. God gives you *exactly* what you need. That means, in your church, this very moment, the right person is present to lead your large group time, help prepare the curriculum, manage the chaos of the two-year-old-room, or even rock babies. If you find your ministry in need of something, God already has anticipated that need and met it— you may just need the discernment to see it.

---

[2] Eugene H. Peterson, *The Message: The Bible in Contemporary Language* (Colorado Springs, CO: NavPress, 2005), Mt 6:25–33.

Resting on Jesus 'promise of complete and total provision is especially hard for those accustomed to spending their lives shopping at Costco and fully filling up their gas tank whenever it's empty. Americans have pulled the rug out from God's feet when it comes to relying on His provision. We are so preoccupied with getting every wish/need granted that we don't even give God credit for what he has given us. We believe the lie that we somehow earned all this ourselves, through hard work. It is not hard to see how that spills over into the way we think about our ministries. Need more leaders? You ask people to serve and if they say yes, ergo, you got those volunteers. We don't let God even be part of the equation, or give him credit for his provision.

When it comes to volunteers, letting God in the driver's seat is a big stretch for many directors and pastors. A majority of kid's ministry workers are struggling to staff their rooms every weekend, so just sitting back and saying "God's got this" seems a like a bit of an oversimplification—like putting a band-aid on an infected limb that's almost beyond saving. We have to see our ministry how God sees it. We have to stop trying to structure our ministry to mimic the church down the street.

God is up in heaven, pleading us to see our ministry the way he sees it because all the resources we need are right in front of us…if we could only see it.

The reason Children's Ministry and Youth Ministry are not one-size-fits-all is because there is no one-size-fits-all church. God brings specific people to specific churches for the benefit of the whole church.

If your church needs someone to operate the computer for worship lyrics, God has already put someone in your church who can do it well.

If your church has a large population of senior adults, God has already put someone in your church who is great at connecting with an older demographic.

If your church has a budget, God has already put someone in your church who is good at handling finances.

If someone donates a pool table to your youth group, God has already put someone in your church who knows how to play.

If you have kids in your church, God has already put someone in your congregation who loves kids and wants to see them be discipled.

It is so important to see what God has given your church. So often, we see all the things that our church is lacking or focus on the negative aspects and church politics. This prevents us from identifying the gifts that God has provided…gifts we need, not gifts we want.

The second part of this idea is that there is a ministry that God wants us to run. This can be tricky to identify because God's vision for your ministry may bear little resemblance to what other ministry experts tell you a ministry should look like. Indeed, the hardest part of trusting God's vision for what your ministry needs to look like is letting go of how things have been done. Like Kylo Ren begging Rey to stop holding on, God is trying to show us a better method with lighter burden. Yet here we sit, frustrated and overwhelmed, feeling lost and alone trying to keep this machine we've inherited running without enough fuel. So, we give more and more of ourselves to compensate, hoping that the next recruiting push, the next new member class, the next ministry fair will tip the scales back into balance.

Not only have I been a children's pastor at a variety of different-sized churches in different parts of the country, I also have the unique perspective of being the child of a children's pastor. For a majority of my childhood and teenage years, I saw my dad giving 110% to his ministry. I lived with the reality of his low pay and long hours. I helped stuff envelopes with letters to new members asking them to consider serving in children's ministry. I attended many summer day camps, VBS weeks, and Christmas pageant rehearsals as a kid and a teenager. Our life revolved around church—often to a fault. I saw the sacrifices my father made to engage kids and I saw that most weeks he had put more energy into other people's families than he did into his own—not because he was a bad father, but because he didn't have help. I really believe my dad was a perfectionist and as a result, he had trouble delegating.

I remember, during my senior year of high school, my dad broke his leg skiing. He had his leg in a full cast up to his hip throughout the spring and summer, including during VBS. One day, he asked me to help him build a set piece for VBS. I come into our garage and there I saw my dad trying to drill two planks together while balancing his broken leg on a chair. I asked him, 'can't someone else do this for you? You're not really ready to be building stuff. 'My dad quickly dismissed that observation. 'It needs to get done this week, 'he said, '…and no one was available.'

It never entered my dad's mind to just not build the set or that he was trying to do something simply because he thought it should be done. In reality, if it didn't get done, VBS would still go on. Sure, maybe this year, VBS would be missing some of the WOW factor, but he wouldn't be hurting himself and suffering silently while the church was oblivious to his sacrifices. Some might call this sacrifice noble and the mark of a true pastor with a good heart. But if this sacrifice is done every month, every year, eventually, carrying a burden alone that God intended to be carried by a team, it will take its toll. My father died of a heart attack only 4 years later. He was only 50 years old.

I always heard people say what a great children's pastor he was. I wonder how much better he would have been if he hadn't done so much of the work himself. I wonder how much more energy he would have had if he had insisted on having an assistant to take some of the ministry responsibilities off his shoulders. If he had a better ministry/family balance I wonder if he would have lived longer.

It can be easy to diagnose this problem from the outside, without any skin in the game. It's much harder when it's your livelihood, your calling, and maybe even your identity. I find myself struggling with the same tendencies toward perfectionism and a desire for excellence in my ministry. I don't want anyone to think I'm lazy or that I don't care. I am being paid to do this, so isn't it kind of cheating to hand responsibilities off to unpaid volunteers?

But then, I look at Jesus 'ministry model. Instead of doing all the healing and casting out demons, he found twelve incompetent volunteers and trained them. (Emphasis on incompetent.) Most of the time, they didn't get it or even worse, they screwed things up, yet Jesus still allowed them to jump right in to the deep end and help him. Even Jesus knew that trying to minister to thousands of people by himself wasn't sustainable, and he definitely knew the message wouldn't be able to reach to the ends of the earth if he was the only one preaching it. Jesus did not create a ministry model that revolved around him. Jesus knew that a model reliant on him doing all the miracles would not last beyond his time on earth. He spent his time demonstrating the power of the Holy Spirit to his disciples and then giving them opportunities to stretch their faith through evangelism, healing and casting out demons. God gave Jesus exactly what he needed: 11 guys who followed him (I don't want to count Judas Iscariot) and eventually put their faith in him that would go on to change the world. God gave Jesus people to stay with and take care of his needs in every town he visited. Jesus didn't have a disciple in charge of accommodations in every town. Jesus rested in the knowledge that God would give him everything he and those with him needed.

There's no story in the Bible that begins with,

Jesus and his disciples had not eaten for many days, for no one was willing to share their food with them.

Or,

On the road to Samaria, Bartholomew collapsed from thirst as he had gone without water for more than a fortnight.

As far as I can tell after studying the Bible, the disciples were always amazed at the abundance of food and wine that God provided through Jesus, as well as the provision of every need, from temple taxes to unridden colts. Doing things God's way meant they never had to worry about having what was needed, they just had to be faithful with what they were entrusted and their needs would be met at the right time.

Perhaps, for many of us, in ministry, it's not that God has failed to provide everything we need, rather, our vision for ministry exceeds what God has provided. Instead of taking a step back and taking stock of what God has given us, we operate with a constant deficiency that leads to burn out. If we were to think of this in business terms, it would be like a business that operates in the red— or always beyond the revenue they have generated. Businesses cannot survive—let alone grow—if they are always outspending their revenue. Healthy organizations operate in the black by not spending more than they have. Businesses that operate in the black understand how to effectively manage their resources and work within what they have to accomplish their mission. So how can we learn to see the resources God has given us and to work with what we have?

CHAPTER
FOUR

BALANCING YOUR VISION WITH REALITY

The movie *Moneyball* tells the true story of Billy Bean, general manager for the Oakland A's, the poorest team in major league baseball. Bean had spent years developing great players through their farm system, resulting in a 2001 playoff berth for the fledgling team, which was led by three-star players. Unfortunately, all of their star players signed with other teams that could pay them far more money going into 2002, and so Billy was left with a skeleton of a team and little money to replace the talents of the departed star players.

Bean unsuccessfully begs the A's owner for the necessary money to attract top-tier baseball talent, leaving him to confront the reality of his situation:

There are rich teams....

there are poor teams...

there's 50 feet of crap... and then there's us.

This forces Billy to think outside the box. Competing major league baseball teams could simply pay huge salaries to elite ball players in order to be competitive, but Oakland can't afford to follow that tried-and-true model for success. So, Bean recruits an assistant GM who helps him identify players based on the mathematical probability that they will earn hits and ignores the advice of Oakland's major league scouts, who have spent decades identifying and developing players. Utilizing statistics, the A's are able to find players that the traditional baseball management system has discarded or overlooked for one reason or another. The 2002 Oakland A's won 20 consecutive games, breaking the MLB record and once again making the postseason—without the help of any star players.

What *Moneyball* demonstrated was an unconventional strategy that was built around the reality of the resources Billy Bean had at his disposal. It would have been easy for Billy to storm out of the owner's meeting complaining that the A's can't win without more money to pay the best players. No one would have thought he was wrong to ask for the same resources all other competing teams had at their fingertips in order to remain competitive.

I really identify with Billy Bean as a children's pastor at a small church. In many ways, it's easy to feel like the Oakland A's while the mega-church down the road is the New York Yankees. It's easy for me to see the resources, teams, and facilities larger churches have and feel like my ministry doesn't compare (or, more painfully, can't *compete*). It's also easy to see a large-church model for doing ministry and feel like there's no way I can pull that off with what God has given me.

I truly believe this focus is why so many children's pastors continue to be frustrated with the limited resources churches give them to minister to kids. Couple that with the reality that corporations are spending BILLIONS of dollars to entertain and market to these same kids, and it's easy to feel overwhelmed and outgunned by our influence.

How am I supposed to engage an 8-year-old boy with tattered puppets and coloring pages when he regularly watches action movies with budgets north of $300,000,000?

How am I supposed to tell a 9-year-old girl that she's the daughter of the King when the fashion industry continues to tell her she's not pretty enough, grown up enough, or desirable enough without their beauty products?

If I want to compete on the same playing field as these juggernauts, I would need millions of dollars and a product that could stand shoulder to shoulder with these companies. We have seen many Christian companies attempt to do this. Some have been more successful than others, but the local church is hardly equipped to throw its hat in the ring of this high-stakes strategy. Disney spent $4.7 billion on marketing in 2020—a year when many of their films were postponed. That's probably more than the combined budget of every Evangelical church in America. And that's just marketing…just getting the word out about their products, parks, and films.

When we admit that we do not have to do events and programming like these multi-billion dollar companies, we can start to ask the really important question:

What can my ministry offer that movies and video games cannot?

Yes, the obvious answer is Jesus and the eternal life we receive when we confess our sins. Let's be careful not to make Jesus a product. Churches shouldn't treat Jesus like Disney treats Mickey Mouse.

When you really deconstruct why a company exists, especially one that exists for kids and teens, their primary reason for existing is to sell something and to get kids attached to a brand. The money isn't in the Spider-Man movie. The money is in the Spider-Man t-shirt, the Spider-Man action figure, the Spider-Man lunch box, the Spider-Man bicycle helmet, and on and on. Companies have gotten so good at this we all expect it. Brands exist to make the brand more money by reaching out in more and more ways.

I think of how this played out in my own life as a young teen. I remember going to the middle school computer lab filled with Macintosh Classic II machines. They were peculiar and boxy, and the mouse only had one button—a much different user experience than my family's IBM computer at home. Apple's bet was that if they gave their computers to schools, kids would become loyal to the brand. Do you think it worked? Go to a college lecture hall and count how many students have forked out a couple grand for MacBooks in comparison to PCs.

What kids may have originally thought was generosity was actually just a long-term form of brand recognition. Every entity kids and teens interact with wants something from them—even when they are giving something away. It's so the customer will eventually buy, subscribe, or invest. Like a "free" game on your phone that gets so difficult you are forced to start paying for the power-ups after a week or two, this is the world of the 21st-century child.

So, if the motivations of companies are purely monetary, how can the Church be different?

How can you create a children's ministry that isn't copying or borrowing from a model built on the monetization of a product and instead build a ministry that is built on a relationship?

When we stop looking at the children's facilities and programming like they are a product, we can begin to rethink how we are using our resources.

What we can all learn from Billy Bean is that when we are faced with the reality of being outspent, we have to look for new ways to execute our vision. Simply asking for more money won't level the playing field.

Congratulations, Captain Obvious! I already know I'm outspent, you might say.

So, what do we do about it?

We leverage the one thing we can give kids and families that Disneyland cannot: **meaningful relationships**. Instead of putting all our energy into creating dazzling spaces or high-energy productions, we need to leverage the power of kids coming into our space and connecting with peers and leaders.

I made some changes in my ministry to facilitate that vision. I had wanted all the kids to connect and be known, and I especially wanted to visit kids to connect with peers whenever possible, but the reality was our kids were not good at befriending kids who were new.

And why was that? As I looked at our elementary space specifically, I realized that the main time for community happened in the 20 minutes or so leading up to the start of service. This is when kids were just hanging out. I had a pre-service loop of interactive videos and music, but it had become background noise to spontaneous games of tag and cliques of kids talking to one another. The reality was that my space was not facilitating connection for new kids. Not only that, it was painfully awkward for kids who were new because they would answer a few questions from other kids and then stand there with nothing to do and nothing else to say. It turns out kids are pretty bad at making small talk. They need facilitated interaction, and they need leaders to model how to interact over and over again.

So, understanding this reality, I had to figure out how to move toward the vision I had. How could we remove the awkwardness? Games! But not monopoly or battleship. These games took too much attention to play and had the potential to make a mess. I found games where 4-8 players could play simultaneously. Everyone is playing at the same time, and the games are easy to learn and join.

We have a foosball table that can accommodate up to 8 kids playing at once. We also got Hungry Hungry Hippos and Mr. Mouth, classic 4-player board games that kids could jump in or out of as their attention span dictated. We also got some games kids had never seen before, like Astro-trash and Pairzi. I resisted the urge to do video games because I wanted games where kids were interacting with each other, not a screen.

This system worked really well. It became much easier for us to get kids to play games together and for us to plug a new kid into a game of foosball or Mr. Mouth with a peer. It then became much easier to talk to a kid because there was something breaking the tension. It's much easier to ask a kid what school they go to while you are both launching bugs into a spinning frog's mouth. It's easier to get kids to bond with a peer if they work together to score a goal. So, this broke the ice and accomplished my vision of building connection between kids—and it didn't cost thousands of dollars or require 10 additional leaders in the room.

Take that, Disneyland!

The most daunting task for any children's director or pastor is recruiting volunteers. I will devote an entire chapter to recruiting, but in the context of reality vs. vision, it's important to be able to see the reality of how you can recruit leaders in relation to other ministries and also try to staff up their departments.

At the beginning of my time at New Life, we had a 4-week discovery class where new people could learn about the church, discover their gifts and strengths, and learn about all the different areas of ministry where they could serve. This culminated in the fourth week, where people could choose the ministry they were most interested in serving. Each pastor sat at a different table, and we invited those in the class to go to the table they were interested in serving. We had our worship pastor, our youth pastor, our connections pastor, our church administrator, our media director, and myself each at a different table. There was a mass exodus to the connections and worship tables. The youth pastor had one or two, and I sat alone, having flashbacks to prom night as I waited for a date that would never show.

It was at this moment I came to understand a tough reality: the conventional way of recruiting at New Life was not going to work for the kid's ministry. And I started to think about why this was a reality. I put myself in the shoes of a new member and began to think about what each ministry was asking of them. People who served in connections typically served one Sunday a month. Most new volunteers held a door open and said hello to people as they came in. A few would serve behind the welcome desk to greet new visitors, and a few others would pass the plates for the offering in service.

Compare this to a volunteer in kids ministry who was expected to serve most, if not every Sunday, possibly change dirty diapers, or endure kids crying for their parents, teach a Bible lesson— sometimes with no additional help in their room—go through an interview with me, pass a background check and have some training before being able to serve.

If I were new and the church leadership had placed a high value on the importance of serving *somewhere*, which area would I choose to serve in? I would most likely choose the easiest ministry that asked the least amount from me. That's just human nature, right? Sure, there are always a few people who see the value in serving with kids or youth or people whom God has already equipped to be in certain roles, but if we present all ministry opportunities side by side and let people choose, we will always find far more people in the areas of ministry that require the least amount of effort. I'm not trying to minimize the greeting ministry. It is a very important first impression for the church, and just because it does not require the same skills as leading a room full of kindergarteners through a Bible lesson does not mean it is without value. But if the culture of our church is simply to "get people serving somewhere" and then assume they will be fulfilled in that role until Jesus returns, we are selling our congregation short.

My *vision* was to have enough volunteers to facilitate grade-specific small groups in each service and have a live worship band and live storytellers. My *reality* was a skeleton crew of committed but maxed-out leaders and a fruitless system for recruiting new children's ministry leaders. As much as I wanted the kids to have close relationships with small group leaders and not have video lessons, it just wasn't going to happen until I found a new way to recruit volunteers.

I went to my senior pastor and expressed my frustration with our format for recruiting leaders through our discovery class. This prompted our staff to rethink our recruitment strategy for new members and make some big changes to the class. We paired down the 4-week class to a one-time class so we didn't lose people over the course of 4 weeks. We cut most of the information on church history and bi-laws and instead gave everyone a packet they could read on their own if that was really important to them. Then, we decided to give each ministry equal time by creating a tour of our ministries through the campus. We would break up the class into groups of 4 or 5 and have them go around to each ministry in the church in their area and hear from that ministry leader about what their ministry was all about. This change proved much more effective because instead of giving a 4-minute lecture to a room of 25 people sitting at tables digesting their lunch, I got to engage a few people at a time who were standing in the kid's area and lay out the vision of the ministry.

I also hardened my pitch for volunteers. This may seem counter-intuitive, but it was probably the most important thing I did when I was recruiting.

For starters, I believe that in any church, children's ministry volunteers are the elite team. The responsibilities and trust we give them are immense—more than a worship leader or even an usher who counts the offering. Kids ministry and student ministry volunteers literally hold the trust of every parent who gives us their child. If that trust is broken, it could spell disaster for the entire church. This is part of why I don't want to come off as desperate and why you shouldn't be desperate, either. When churches get desperate for children's ministry volunteers, we can invite a wolf into the pasture without realizing it. When we compromise and bend our own policies in order to onboard a few leaders, we make our ministries vulnerable to abuses from the wrong kinds of leaders. That reality has far-reaching consequences, and I have to guard against those consequences before I attempt to move forward toward a vision.

So, my pitch to everyone basically goes like this:

The Children's Ministry team is the navy seals of volunteers at our church. We don't take just anybody. Our leaders are the most trained, most trusted, most vetted leaders in the church because we value our kids here, and what we do has eternal consequences. There are two really important roles where I'm looking for the right people… (then I would describe these roles and what is unique or important about those roles. And then I'd say…) *if you think kids ministry is in your wheelhouse, then your first step is to fill out this application, and then we will schedule a time to meet.*

Viola! I started getting 1 or 2 applications at the end of each class. Does that sound like I'm drowning in volunteers? No. But the point is not to be drowning in volunteers who are joining for the wrong reasons. I had to shift my focus from what I didn't have to what God was providing me. I had to make changes based on what I had to work with while not compromising the standards I had for those who were serving with kids. To return to the baseball analogy, I still had to field a team, but I wasn't going to field a team of horrible players. I had to figure out how to play baseball with 6 players and recruit my way up to a full team. I still needed to be the gatekeeper, and an unintended benefit was that parents who went through our discovery class saw that I was serious about the kids' ministry and about getting the right leaders. I had more support from families when they saw that I made finding the right leaders to invest in their kids a priority over having a warm body and plugging a hole in our team.

But changing our church-wide recruitment system was only half the battle. I would never find enough leaders by only recruiting a few volunteers from our new members' class every 3 or 4 months. Little did I know that God had a large number of volunteers waiting for me to invite them to be involved.

CHAPTER FIVE

USING WHAT YOU HAVE EFFECTIVELY

As our kid's ministry began experiencing rapid growth, we quickly found ourselves short-staffed with unsafe ratios. What do I mean by rapid growth? When I started, we were averaging 2-3 babies (children under 2) between 2 services. In the space of 18 months, we were suddenly averaging 7-8 babies PER service. I'm not going to spend any time in this chapter explaining why a young church has an influx of babies or making connections between a rare Georgia blizzard that happened the year before, but thanks to a remodel of our pre-k rooms and shuffling around the age groups into different rooms, we were able to accommodate more babies than we ever had before. The tough part is, you won't see a large influx without first having room to contain it.

You may be asking *"how can my church see an influx of babies like this?"*

First, pray for a blizzard. Then, apply the concept of the Law of the Room to your current ministry. You may have experienced this phenomenon in your ministry already and not know it.

A few years and a mega-church job earlier, our Saturday night services would break out elementary kids into grade-specific rooms for small group time. We had 6 rooms, but one room was significantly smaller than the other spaces. We chose to put our second graders in this room as we averaged 15 second graders. The room could hold about 15 kids and 2 leaders, depending on the setup. As we tracked attendance, we noticed an interesting phenomenon: One week, the room would hit 18 kids, then the next week, attendance would drop down to around 10. Over the next few weeks, numbers would steadily climb back to 18 and then drop down back to 10 the next week. This happened over the course of about 4 months again and again. We realized we were encountering the law of the room. Since the room was only designed to fit 15 kids, parents would come and pick up their kids and see how crowded the room was. The next week, they would either not come or attend another service because of the jam-packed room. The parents that picked up their kids once the room had emptied out a bit didn't see these conditions, and so thought nothing of it.

We knew that our leader was dynamic and creative and had a great gift at connecting with these kids, so we appealed to the church leadership to move the adult discipleship group using a nearby space to other rooms in order to open up a larger room. Once we moved that 2nd grade class to a larger room, it was soon averaging 40 kids. We hadn't changed our marketing strategy, our curriculum, or the leader, but we had given the leader more room to work with (and subsequently, more helpers as the class grew). It took some good old-fashioned church politics but came from what was most effective. It was an easy sell to our church leadership to open up space for more families. That discipleship class had around 20 adults sitting at tables using a room that we could put 50 kids in. Was it the most effective use of space? Yes. Were there pros and cons? Definitely. Were a few of the adults a bit flustered about meeting in another room on the other side of campus? Naturally. When all was said and done, we ended up netting 25 more 2nd graders and their families as a result.

I have worked in many churches of many different sizes, and I've seen this law of the room play out in every kid's ministry.

Only when we look at all the options and find a creative way to solve the problem, do we begin to use what we have effectively? I have also seen many churches beating their heads against a wall, saying, I don't understand why we are maxing out at _____ number of kids? The law of the room probably has some part to play in the reason.

At the fertile church in Georgia where I served (around 500 people), our nursery was essentially a closet when I was hired. There was about a five-foot-by-five-foot space for babies to play when accounting for the gliders, changing tables, and other baby gear. I quickly realized the reason we weren't seeing many babies in our nursery was because the space was just not usable as a nursery...or really, for anything. The room could only truly accommodate 1 baby and 1 leader without parents feeling like their babies were packed in like sardines.

In the coming months, we embarked on a renovation of our kid's space, and my biggest priority was expanding that room into a usable classroom. We sacrificed our children's ministry lobby space, built some walls, tore down another, and ended up with a decent size room that could accommodate 6 babies. And in a matter of weeks after completing the remodel, we were averaging 4-5 babies per service. I began to realize we would soon run into the same problem again with the room size. So, I began looking for another solution. We had 4 rooms for our pre-k and nursery, with different age groups in each room. Ironically, our smallest class (5-year-olds) had the biggest room, and our biggest class (3s and 4s) had our square-shaped room (most of the rooms in our kid's area were long, skinny rectangles probably designed by Satan himself.)

When I looked at the design of our rooms, we weren't using our space effectively. In fact, the only reason our 5-year-olds were in the largest room was simply *because they had always been.* We did a round of musical classrooms and ended up swapping all our age groups into new rooms. Once we moved babies into a bigger room, we were averaging 8 or 9 babies per service. Again, the law of the room allowed us to accommodate more.

Look for ways to maximize your space by asking other leaders what they would do. Your space solutions may be staring you right in the face, and you just simply never thought to do it that way. And don't be afraid to talk to leaders about switching rooms. There are plenty of leaders who have served for many and may have become attached to a certain room for one reason or another. The real question is, how can you help them see the bigger picture beyond their group of kids or their space? It is so important that you do not just blow through the door and tell them bluntly, "We're moving your class." That's a quick way to alienate your leaders.

I found one of the best ways to approach volunteers about space problems was to just come to them with the dilemma.

"Suzy, how has your class been doing? ...Have you noticed how packed the 3-year-old room has been the last few weeks? I'm trying to figure out what to do. I feel like we can't let any more kids in that room safely."

Now, if this is an amazing, selfless volunteer, they may jump right in and suggest switching rooms, and then, they look like the hero—which is what you should want anyway.

In ministry, it's always important to let your volunteers be the hero whenever possible. Did they just echo your idea to the senior pastor? It was their idea. He/she is such a great problem solver. Did they just talk to another leader about ways they can alleviate overcrowding? Praise them for thinking about the needs of the ministry.

Only when you're secure in your own leadership can you allow yourself to pass the credit and praise on to your team. Your senior pastor isn't stupid (hopefully). He or she can see your leadership, mindset, and attitude trickling down to the entire team, and that will reflect well on you. But what does not reflect well is when a conflict between two kids' ministry leaders who are arguing about rooms and space makes it back to your lead pastor. Those are not fun meetings.

It breaks my heart to see different ministries in churches *fighting* over rooms. I wish I could say it doesn't happen, but it most certainly does. People may not understand the law of the room, but almost everyone can understand the value of having a desirable room to meet in. Many youth or kids ministry leaders can understand the resentment that starts to build when you are desperate for space and another ministry is monopolizing it. Many times, our ministries seem to be in competition with one another—whether for resources, space, visibility, or leaders—and we lose sight of the fact we are all on the same team, working toward the same goal.

What about your team? What are some ways you can use your volunteers, or volunteer pool, more effectively?

As the growth of the kids' ministry outpaced my ability to recruit, I fervently asked God for more leaders. In response, God opened my eyes to see a population I had pretty much written off—young teens. Many of our middle schoolers had come up through our ministry and wanted to stay connected, but I had told many of them they needed to wait until they were in high school as I felt they were too young to handle the responsibility. God really convinced me to not underestimate this age group. What I needed was a way to make sure the middle schoolers were actually benefitting our adult leaders and not just adding to their responsibilities by putting another kid they had to supervise. How would I make sure these teens would benefit the ministry they wanted to serve? In response, I created a training wheels trial period for any volunteer under 16.

If a student wants to serve in a kid's ministry, I require a parent to serve with them for 1-3 months. Most parents see the benefit in their child volunteering and are willing to make a short-term commitment so that their son or daughter can benefit from volunteering. I make sure there is a fairly good age gap between the student leader and the room they're serving in. (I won't put a 6th or 7th grader in an elementary room, for example. And I won't have certain personalities serve in the nursery with babies.) After each service in which the student and parent serve, I check in with the team lead from that room and ask how things went. Ninety-nine percent of the time, the feedback has been really positive. After a few more weeks of serving, I ask the team lead if they feel the student is ready to take off the training wheels and serve without their parent. For the final week, I have the student serve without the parent and have the parent at the check-in desk or help with snacks, etc. If all goes well, the student leader is cleared to serve without their parent.

This system has done a few really important things:

It allows me to say yes to younger volunteers serving when I used to say *not yet*.

It empowers younger leaders in our church by giving them a place to serve.

It gives me a pool of background-checked adult leaders that I can ask to substitute or serve in VBS or special events.

It creates a farm system, helping to develop younger leaders in our church—and that benefits the whole congregation for years to come.

What is a farm system, you may ask? The farm system is another sports team analogy. Every major league team has minor league affiliates where they send their younger players to develop and grow. Baseball and hockey both have multiple levels of minor league teams connected with their NHL or MLB teams. When teams draft young players, those players will spend some time in the farm system, working to hopefully get their shot at the major league positions. The idea is that there is a system for developing talent "in-house" rather than always having to find it outside the organization.

A young player in the ECHL has a long way to go before he is a starter on the NHL team, but if his skills develop, he will move up to the AHL, where the crowds are bigger and the stakes are higher. Then, if he proves himself there, he may get called up to the NHL.

The farm system is a very important concept to get behind if you want to increase the total number of volunteers in your church.

Yes, I had a bunch of younger volunteers who were helpful but not able to lead a room by themselves when they started. But look, 4 years forward, and I now have a large group of 16 and 17-year-old leaders who have spent years working with kids and have transitioned into small group leader roles for elementary kids.

I wanted a vibrant small group strategy for our elementary classes when I started, but I could never get enough leaders to keep this consistent. So, I had to *farm* my way into that vision and grow leaders who could accomplish this strategy a few years down the road. That's what evaluating your ministry is all about—finding the best way to use what you have now and ways to get where God wants you to be. It

CAN YOU FARM YOUR WAY INTO THE VISION YOU HAVE FOR THE FUTURE OF YOUR MINISTRY?

may not be what you envisioned or what other churches are able to do, but God might just have all your staffing solutions right in front of you if you submit to His methods and His timetable.

Another farm system example is to use a more holistic approach to developing leaders in your church. I've always said that children's ministry volunteers are the Navy Seals of volunteers in every church; they are the most vetted, most highly trained, most trusted, and (should be) the most exclusive ministry in the church. For this reason, it can be very challenging to simply recruit anyone off the pew to serve.

I am a product of a farm system in ministry, and it wasn't exactly a straight line to where I am now.

When I was in middle school, I started playing drums for the student worship team. I'm pretty sure I was way too loud and more than likely playing out of time. I still remember the first time I played in front of the youth group. We played Big House by Audio Adrenaline (that should give you an idea of how long ago this was).

For the next 5 years, I regularly played drums in the worship teams for middle and high school. As my playing improved, I moved up to the main services, all the while falling more in love with music and performance. I eventually decided to study percussion performance in college, and I spent most Sundays of my college career playing at one church or another. In my second or third year of college, the worship leader of our Intervarsity chapter stepped down. The rest of us on the team were asked if any of us felt called to lead the team. At that moment, I realized God wanted me to take the step to move into a leadership role and stretch myself. By that point, everyone acknowledged that my drumming skills were top-notch, but a drumming worship leader? How would that work? The general consensus among the team was that I should stick to what I was good at and not try to stretch myself. But luckily for me, the director of our chapter saw potential in me to be more and graciously allowed me to lead worship. (He still appointed a co-leader for me to work with, though.)

There was a steep learning curve as I had to sing and play drums at the same time— which most drummers will tell you is no small feat. But it was so energizing to feel God stretching my talents and leadership abilities. I look back now and realize I must have been a pill to work with and had very little grace or patience with those I was leading, but we all have to start somewhere, right?

The following summer, I heard about an internship in the Artist Community of the church I had been attending. I figured this would be a great way for me to really investigate whether worship leading was where God wanted me, so I applied and somehow was accepted. Granted, this was the unpaid internship I mentioned earlier that paid me in experience and the occasional free lunch, but I see that internship as the catalyst to my career in ministry.

Imagine if the opportunity for me to move into leading the worship team had been closed off to me? Imagine what my life would be like now if people saw my percussive abilities and never asked more of me or developed my other abilities? Where would I be now? I'm sure if you and I could sit down and have coffee, you could tell me a similar story about how you got into ministry. There is a development process, and the sooner churches embrace this process, the more skilled leaders they will have at their disposal. But you don't get those well-developed leaders right away.

Time and time again, in the Bible, we see God developing leaders. Think of Joseph or Moses, Peter or Paul. How detrimental would it have been to the Kingdom of God if none of these leaders were developed and asked to do more than they were doing? Joseph would have kept running Potiphar's household in Egypt, his name forgotten. Moses would have tended sheep in the desert. Peter would have continued to catch fish, and Saul would have stayed a legalistic teacher of the law who faded into obscurity shortly after his death.

God has established a farm system, and it involves those who have come up through the ranks to continue developing new leaders. He brings rough, uncut gems into our ministries, and it's our job as pastors to help cut them into beautiful gems for God's crown of glory. It's a leader's job not just to keep those we lead busy in a role but to develop them into something more so that when they look back twenty years, they see how their gifts and skills were developed and matured for the benefit of the Church. Does it take time to mine and cut a precious gem? Of course. But is its value increased when we do that? Yes, it is.

If I had been allowed to simply play drums week in and week out, after 20 years, I would be left feeling unfulfilled and underutilized because where I started was not where God ultimately wanted me to end up.

Why do we sell our volunteers short by having that expectation of them in various ministries? Am I expecting that pre-k teacher to keep teaching that class for 30 years and never ask more of her? Is that fair to our people? But this is exactly what happens more often than not. We get someone in a role that is comfortable, and for fear of losing them or having to replace them, we keep them there.

Jesus had a great parable to address this in Matthew 25:14- 30 NIV.**14** "For it will be like a man going on a journey, who called his servants and entrusted to them his property. **15** To one, he gave five talents, to another two, to another one, to each according to his ability. Then he went away. **16** He who had received the five talents went at once and traded with them, and he made five talents more. **17** So also he who had the two talents made two talents more. **18** But he who had received the one talent went and dug in the ground and hid his master's money. **19** Now, after a long time, the master of those servants came and settled accounts with them. **20** And he who had received the five talents came forward, bringing five talents more, saying, 'Master, you delivered to me five talents; here, I have made five talents more.' **21** His master said to him, 'Well done, good and faithful servant. You have been faithful over a little; I will set you over much. Enter into the joy of your master.' **22** And he also who had the two talents came forward, saying, 'Master, you delivered to me two talents; here, I have made two talents more.' **23** His master said to him, 'Well done, good and faithful servant. You have been faithful over a little; I will set you over much. Enter into the joy of your master.' **24** He also who had received the one talent came forward, saying, 'Master, I knew you to be a hard man, reaping where you did not sow, and gathering where you scattered no seed, **25** so I was afraid, and I went and hid your talent in the ground. Here, you have what is yours.' **26** But his master answered him, 'You wicked and slothful servant! You knew that I reaped where I had not sown and gathered where I scattered no seed? **27** Then you ought to have invested my money with the bankers, and at my coming, I should have received what was my own with interest. **28** So take the talent from him and give it to him who has the ten talents. **29** For to everyone who has will more be given, and he will have an abundance. But from the one who has not, even what he has will be taken away. **30** And cast the worthless servant into the outer darkness. In that place, there will be weeping and gnashing of teeth.'

Matthew 25:14-30[3]

---

[3] The Holy Bible, New International Version (Grand Rapids, Michigan: Zondervan, 1973) Mt. 25:14-30

Many people read this and think Jesus is talking about investments or giving, but what he's really talking about is developing the investments of the Kingdom of God. Developing the strengths and skills of people in our churches has to be seen as a long-term investment in the life of the Church. Too often, the "professional Christians" exclude lay persons from doing the significant work of the church and reduce their role to that of a helper. We have the opportunity to increase the talents we are given, but instead, we bury them in the ground. And we wonder why church attendance and engagement are on the decline! We have been lulling our members to sleep by asking so little of them year after year.

"But Brian, you don't see my volunteers! They work their rear-ends off. We have leadership teams and mission committees and all sorts of ways for people to step up!"

If you are already doing this-awesome! Keep doing it. But here's where I'm going to make things tense during the staff meeting...

What if we treat the easier volunteer positions like greeting, coffee, parking, etc., like a farm system? What if we let people prove themselves in these ministries and then meet with them and challenge them to do something more than shake hands or pass out coffee?

Don't get me wrong, churches need people to shake hands and make coffee, but at what point do we see the value in developing hand shakers and coffee makers into small group leaders or scheduling coordinators? Greeting ministry, coffee ministry, media ministry, and parking ministry are all important parts of the church, and each of these areas should have their own paths for growth, but what if we see paths for growth that go outside the silos we've created for each ministry team?

Yeah, this system could easily be construed as elitist, placing greater importance on some ministry's volunteers over others, but if we cast the right vision for it, we don't have to see it that way. A farm system for volunteering has to start with leaders not being territorial with their volunteers, and that's not easy to do. As we know, volunteers are scarce—not just in children's and youth ministries but in virtually all ministries—so we are competing for a scarce resource with other leaders who have their own volunteer needs.

This idea is a seismic shift in how churches operate. There may be a few leaders who serve on more than one team or committee, but to really embrace this strategy would require support from every ministry leader.

Once we start acting like kid's ministry volunteers are the Navy Seals of volunteers in every church, the sooner your team will have more pride in the ministry that happens in their classrooms. There could be some amazing leaders—some uncut gems—serving in other places in the church that are ready to be called into kid's ministry. Of course, the most important part of having a successful farm system is having a way to train new leaders so they are not overwhelmed or intimidated. We will get into that in a later chapter.

So, there's my ground-breaking idea: plunder the greeting and media ministries for volunteers! What a great way to alienate everyone you work with, right?

Obviously, you have to be diplomatic and honoring of other leaders and ministries. This is a church-wide strategy that all the leaders need to be on board with. Plenty of great churches have been developing and farming leaders for decades. It's not a foreign concept, but it also doesn't happen by accident. What you have to do is find a way to help other leaders in your church see developing leaders as a win. If they already do, then it should be an easy sell, but don't be naive in thinking you can just approach volunteers in other ministries and not face some repercussions.

CHAPTER SIX

RECRUITING

One of the biggest obstacles to having a robust team of volunteers is recruiting. If you're anything like me on a Sunday or weekend, you're not exactly standing around shooting the breeze. Whether you're filling in for an absent teacher, dealing with an unruly kid, trying to get the stupid printer to print, or maybe getting a minute to actually connect with a kid or parent about home life, Children's Pastors don't get much downtime. The hectic needs of ministry create a huge challenge when it comes to being available to recruit new leaders. You have so many priorities in that brief window after service when you can connect with families before they rush off to the rest of their day that talking to people about serving is nearly impossible.

Real Life Volunteer Stories

Years ago, I had a new volunteer named Hein. He had never taught preschoolers, but he was willing to learn and even said that once trained he'd be happy to be a teacher in the room. The first week he was scheduled with a veteran teacher, so that she could do some on the job training with him. But that morning I got a call from the teacher. She had a sick kid and wasn't coming. We were short staffed all around and I had to make a spur of the moment decision: I grabbed an extra helper from a different age group and gave Hein a 2-minute orientation – here's the lesson, here's the schedule, that kid can't have snacks, call me if you need anything – then I threw him into the deep end.

Honestly, I was convinced that he would be scared away and would never want to serve again. I believed this to be a huge failure on my part. Half an hour later, I peeked in the class window and it was the most organized two-year-old class I had ever seen. I was in shock.

At the end of the class, I complimented him on his classroom management skills and asked his secret. I'll never forget his response: He followed the schedule. I was thankful that we had a schedule in the room and was reminded that a schedule can be the difference between chaos and actual teaching.

Not only did Hein continue to serve, but he told me that morning was proof to him that God would equip him for the role, and a few months later Hein stepped up in a leadership position in the preschool department. He told me a few years later, after the birth of their first child that serving in children's ministry helped to equip him as a parent as he learned from the other teachers and parents in the church.

Bethany Darwin

Evangelical Church of Dubai

Dubai, United Arab Emirates

With this in mind, I try to make the most of other church events where I'm not juggling many responsibilities. Does your church do potlucks or brunches? Make sure you take advantage of the opportunity to talk to various people about serving in kid's ministry. These types of settings are great because you can take a bit more time to get to know someone and not be seen as pushy and only interested in recruiting them for your ministry.

That is one bonus of having some kind of regular way to recruit from a new members class, like I mentioned earlier, with our discovery class. I have a distraction-free environment to "sell" serving in my ministry. However, if I depended solely on recruiting from a membership class, I would be missing some church members who have a stronger connection to the church and possibly the ministry itself.

Even though it seems obvious, it needs to be said that the very best place to start your recruiting process is on your knees. Ask God to bring certain people to mind. Remember, God knows what you need. You may have overlooked someone who is incredibly qualified or passionate. On the other end, God may start prompting certain people to seek me out about volunteering. I remember being in prayer about who God wanted me to talk to. God brought a certain parent to mind that I had kind of written off because she seemed so over-extended. Her son played baseball and had frequent out-of-town games on the weekends.

Before I go on, let me just say your recruiting pitch (or whatever you would like to call it) should be simple and direct. If you've ever worked in sales, you'll know there are a few steps in the process of getting someone to commit. And most of the time, whether you're selling used cars, vacuum cleaners, timeshares, or a private college education, customers are buying because of you, not just because of the product. It may seem crass to equate recruiting leaders in kid's ministry with buying a used car. So how is it similar? You need to understand the *why* behind the *what*.

Your new volunteer cannot be just a number. You cannot see them as another cog in your ministry machine. You are not trying to fill a spot with their warm body; you are trying to reveal why serving in the kid's ministry is significant and why it will be so satisfying for them. You need to help people realize the kingdom impact of your ministry, and you need to tie it all back to your vision. This can be incredibly hard to do if you're talking to someone you have just met or a group of new members who are blankly staring back at you.

Have you ever encountered a salesperson who is pushy or manipulative? Someone you know is a total jerk when he or she is not talking to a potential sale, and who doesn't see you as a person but just another number toward winning that trip to Cancun? That is *not* the kind of feeling I want people to have when I talk to them about serving. Serving in my ministry should not make anyone feel used or like they are serving out of guilt. I've seen some pastors and ministry leaders 'heap on the guilt—like these kids are going to burn in hell unless you sign on this dotted line and show up next Sunday. While some people might believe this is a true statement, don't lead with that. It's in poor taste to motivate your team out of guilt, and it makes you come off as manipulative. You have God in your corner. You don't need to resort to manipulation or coercion to get people to serve. Using coercion and manipulation will only build a team of wishy-washy leaders who are there for all the wrong reasons and who will flee at the first sign of trouble or hardship.

Write out and rehearse your "sales pitch" about serving before you recruit. You need to be able to simply and passionately relay your vision for the ministry and why they need to be a part of it. If you are truly passionate about what you're doing, it won't be that hard to do. Parents are very good at picking up on false motives— they have kids crying out loud! Don't try to con people into serving in your ministry. Start simply by praying. Ask God to bring certain people to mind. You might know them, you might not, but nine times out of ten, you will need to approach them. A handful of people will come to you, but many are wrestling with the Holy Spirit internally and really just need you to confirm what God has been speaking to them. When you ask God who He wants you to talk to, amazing things happen.

So, I approached that parent with a super busy schedule, expecting to get shot down.

Me: Hey Julie, I was praying for parents who could serve in kids' ministry, and God brought you to mind. Have you ever thought about serving in kids ministry?

Julie:You know what, I've been thinking about it for a while. Our schedule is just so crazy, and I don't want to say I'll serve only to be gone most Sundays.

Me:I totally respect that. I do have other ways you could serve outside of Sunday mornings.

Julie:Really?

Me:Yeah! I'm always looking for committed leaders on Wednesday Nights, and I can always help prep curriculum during the week.

Julie:I think I could make Wednesdays work most weeks.

Me:That would be amazing! Let me give you an application to fill out. I'd also like to set up a time to meet and talk about serving. What's your schedule like this week or next?

Boom.

It's not always going to go that smoothly, but I was amazed in that particular situation how God met a need I had on Wednesday Nights—a time that is always difficult to get adult leaders—when I had written Julie off.

When you ask God to bring people to mind, trust that God has been stirring in that person's heart as well. In Julie's case, she had spent a year wrestling with God about serving because she knew it was important to give back to her church. But she saw her hectic schedule on the weekends as preventing her from doing anything at all. I had to help her make the connection of serving on Wednesday nights as an option.

The other thing I do is outline some concrete action steps as we finish talking. Julie has two: filling out the application and finding a time to meet with me. It's easiest for me to try and land on a time while we're talking in person. Otherwise, we could spend weeks going back and forth, trying to find a day and time that works. With most people, I hand them an application, and then once I get it back, I schedule an interview. But in cases like this, it's certainly okay to get an interview on the calendar to save yourself a few weeks. My expectation is that the application will be done by our meeting.

One great piece of ministry advice I learned was that it's best to give people two options for meeting. Ask if he or she is available any mornings or afternoons. Once you find a day or time of day, look at your schedule and give them two options: "You can do Mondays, ok? I've got a 10 AM or 4 PM; which one works for you?"

Nothing is more frustrating to me than going back and forth on days and times to meet. There were plenty of working adults who simply didn't have time during working hours, so I tried to make sure I had one weeknight evening slot to offer in those cases.

Out of all the challenges children and youth pastors face, recruiting quality leaders for your ministry is usually at the top of the list. If you struggle to find an efficient way to recruit leaders from your church, you are not alone. (Not to mention that once word gets out that you are trying to recruit, people stop making eye contact with you in the lobby or hide behind plants and furniture.) It can be easy to get discouraged.

While you're discouraged, let me take this opportunity to further your sense of despair: you may be tempted to ask someone in kids ministry who is already serving somewhere else. I had one volunteer who was actively serving on four teams. FOUR! She sang on the worship team, served as a greeter, led a small group, and was a leader in our toddler room. Not only did this impact her ability to participate in a worship service, but it also made scheduling her very difficult. I had to check with two other ministries just to make sure she was available to serve in the kids' ministry. And if a vocalist called out for a Sunday and she was asked to step in, you can guess which ministry won that contest.

While you may be feeling desperate, it's never a good idea to ask someone to take on multiple roles at your church if that person is already plugged in. There are plenty of people who say yes to everything that's asked of them. Perhaps this yes-saying church member's motives are pure, and they are serving for all the right reasons, but when we go for the low-hanging fruit of people who always say yes, a few different things happen:

You are adding another thing to their full plate—making him or her less effective overall.

You miss giving people on the fringes of your church a way to connect through serving by asking someone who is already committed in other areas.

At the beginning of this book, I shared the results of a few polls I took among children's pastors and directors, and the common theme is that most of the leaders in children's and youth ministries feel overwhelmed by the lack of help they have, coupled with the expectations of the ministry. These feelings easily cause discouragement, especially when other ministries seem to be drowning in volunteers or require very few to function well.

As I have said in earlier chapters, I believe children's ministry volunteers are the Navy Seals of volunteers in the church, and as such, this shapes how I recruit leaders. I don't have to give you specific examples of what can happen when you get desperate for anyone with a pulse and let someone serve in your ministry who you know shouldn't be there. The news loves to cover stories of abuse and predatory behavior within churches, and it has hurt our witness to the community and to our world when families don't trust us. There was a time when churches were naive about the motives of those who wanted to serve in kids' and youth ministries, and most of them paid a high price for that blind trust.

As the head of your ministry area, you, first of all, have to be the gatekeeper. You have to let the Holy Spirit speak to you about every potential volunteer and not ignore red flags simply because you need another leader. Remember, God gives you *exactly* what you need, even if it seems impossible to do what is asked of you with what you have. When we rest on this knowledge, we can say no to people who, for one reason or another, set off that alarm bell in our gut.

NEVER LET DESPERATION FOR VOLUNTEERS ALLOW YOU TO LOWER YOUR STANDARDS JUST TO KEEP A ROOM OPEN OR A SMALL GROUP GOING.

What do I mean by this?

At the large church I served at, we would encourage prospective volunteers to come by the kids' area and observe what we did. We had a system in place for people to observe in a room, where we would give them a red lanyard and pair them with a current leader who would keep an eye on them—making sure the future leader didn't have direct contact with any children but also could get an idea of what serving in kids ministry looked like.

One day, a young man, we'll call him Fritz, came up to the kid's area and said, "I was told this is where I can be with the kids." Right away, there was a bit of a red flag in how Fritz talked about being with kids, but I gave him the benefit of the doubt.

"Are you interested in serving in the kid's ministry?" I asked.

"Definitely," Fritz replied. Fritz was in his mid-20s, and right away, I didn't have a great feeling about him. I could not point to anything with certainty after a 10-second conversation, but there were many other potential volunteers who did not set off alarm bells in our first encounter.

I proceeded to explain our observation system and what he could expect. I gave him a red observer tag and paired him with Aya, one of my trusted 4th-grade leaders. I introduced Fritz to her and gave her a few minutes to explain what her role was as a 4th-grade team lead and let him see how she set up her room, etc.

When the kids broke out into grades, I accompanied the 4th graders to their room so I could check in with Fritz as everyone settled into the room. I hung around for a few minutes and then proceeded to check on other rooms and leaders. As the service wrapped up, I came back to the 4th grade room, where Fritz was still observing from the back of the room. As we walked back to the volunteer lounge, I asked him what he thought. He had good things to say and was complimentary of Aya and the way she led her class.

Normally, I would give potential volunteers an application as their next step to fill out and bring back, but something inside told me to wait. I told Fritz we would send him an application at a later date, thanked him for wanting to serve, and sent him on his way. Then, I checked back in with Aya at the end of the service.

"So, what did you think of Fritz?" I asked.

"Well, he seemed ok," she replied. I could sense a bit of hesitation, so I pressed her a bit.

"What did you *really* think of him?"

Aya replied, "Honestly, he kind of creeped me out." That was all the confirmation I needed to not let Fritz go any further in the process of serving in our ministry.

Is that judgmental? *Yes, it is.*

Is that excluding someone that might end up being a good volunteer? *Yep.*

Did I have any proof that he was a risk to the kids in our ministry *besides an uneasy feeling shared between a female leader and me? Nope.*

Is this system fair to Fritz? *Nope.*

It is important to understand the sacred duty you have to protect the kids in your ministry at all costs. Like it or not, we are a candy store for some very sick and evil people, and if we don't do everything we can to keep the wolves away from our sheep, then we are doing all the kids in our ministry a grave disservice that could scar them for life.

Don't ignore that uneasy feeling in your gut when you know something is off. I believe women have a much finer-tuned sense of a person's character than men do; that's why I checked in with Aya and got her honest feedback. Men can hone this sense over time, but the first thing you have to do is give yourself permission to make a snap judgment about someone. You have to pay more attention to the Holy Spirit than the needs of your volunteer schedule.

Never put yourself in a place where you are so desperate that you lower the standards you have in place to protect the kids in your ministry just to keep a room open.

As a result, in children's ministry, we *have to* judge people. We judge people who want to serve. We judge people loitering around the kid's classrooms. We even have to judge if a parent or guardian is a danger to their child (but that's a whole other book). I'd rather be overly cautious than overly trusting and end up in an interview on 60 Minutes trying to explain why I didn't see the warning signs in a particular volunteer because I was so desperate for help.

The Navy Seals don't have an open call. That's part of what makes them elite, and that's part of the prestige that comes with being a Navy Seal—not everyone makes it. You can't say children's ministry is *the elite ministry* and then beg for help from the stage on a Sunday morning.

Again, if we believe God has and will give us *exactly* what we need, then we don't have to beg—we need to trust in God's provision and trust that what God has given us is enough.

So, when we recruit, should we give an impassioned plea from the stage during the worship service? No.

Well, great, Brian, now you've made it even harder to get leaders! Thanks for the advice!

There is a better way to recruit, but trying to just run out and recruit without first having a system to transform these recruits into regularly serving volunteers will make it harder in the long run. Before you recruit anyone, the first thing you need is an onboarding system in your ministry. Mine works like this:

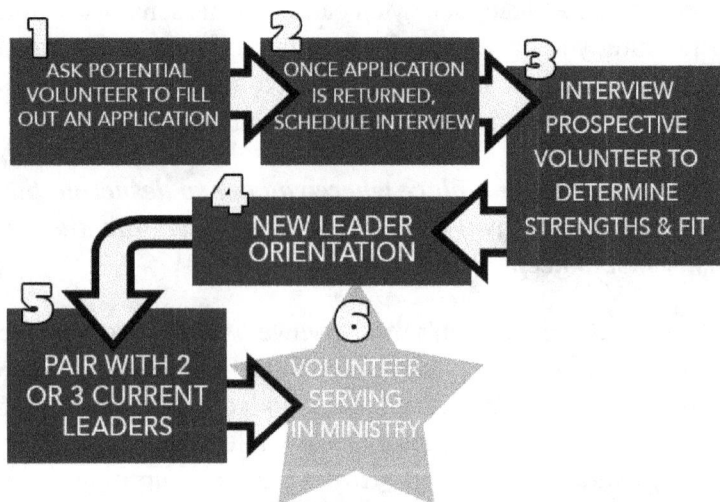

The best recruiting begins with a system already in place for taking someone from a prospective volunteer to a committed volunteer. Your system doesn't have to be exactly like mine, but you need a process in place before you just start asking people to serve in your ministry. That is, unless you like being very excited that you finally found a great leader for that particular class, but as they begin volunteering, they miss a Sunday, then another, and then just ghost you completely. Then, when you see them in church, they pretend they can't speak English and run to their car.

For a few years after college, I worked as an admissions counselor for a private university in Colorado. For any given semester, I would have to manage between two to three thousand prospective students. Some were just clicking around on the internet and had little real interest in taking all the necessary steps to go to college, and others were ready to start right away. It was my job to identify serious students who were ready for the rigors of college and move them through the application and registration process. There are many parallels between identifying prospective college students and prospective volunteers in your ministry.

Why do colleges have an application in the first place? Applications exist to separate a casual student from a serious one. Completing an application tells the school a couple of very important things they want to know:

I can finish a task

I can think critically

I know how to use a computer

I am serious enough about this application to set aside time to complete it.

I know how to follow instructions.

Obviously, the information in the application is important as well, but the actual process of wanting to complete, then completing, and finally returning an application for serving in your ministry tells you right away that this person can do everything on the list. There have been some people I have talked to about serving, and they say, "Oh, I really want to serve," but they can't do the simple task of filling out a 2-page application that is mostly questions about themselves. If I were to just let that volunteer serve anyway, I would be constantly frustrated for one of the aforementioned reasons on this list.

The application is the first gate that volunteers need to get through to serve in my children's ministry, and it is 100% on them to complete it. I may remind them if it's been a few weeks and they still haven't gotten it back to me. I'll give them a hard copy if they want to do it that way, but if I don't get an application, I won't move forward with that person. The Holy Spirit may use this gate to keep many people from serving who would not end up benefiting the ministry.

Not everyone is going to say yes immediately. Children's ministry can be a bit intimidating, especially for those who don't have kids or younger siblings. Trying to pressure someone into "just trying it" is a one-way ticket to quit town. There are people who need to know what they're getting into because they don't want to get in over their head and feel overwhelmed.

I usually do not use the term interview, because it can make people needlessly nervous, but for all intents and purposes, you are interviewing them for this volunteer position. You are setting aside about an hour to get to know this person and their story and also let them get to know you and your ministry. It's also the time when you can head off any fears or misconceptions they might have about serving in your ministry.

I always tell new volunteers, "I'm not going to throw you into a room by yourself with 10 kids and some curriculum. I'm going to pair you with other leaders so you can see how they do it and what works. You will not be thrown to the wolves."

This reassurance can be tremendously important as you meet with prospective volunteers. Many people are afraid that they will be expected to just wing it with a bunch of kids in a room by themselves. This exact scenario may have played out with their own Sunday school leader in the past. If that were the case, I wouldn't want to serve in that environment either. Maybe the expectations were too high when they served somewhere else in the past, and they didn't want to get burned again. It's your job to communicate that things are running well, and you won't ask more of them than they are ready or able to give.

The perspective of someone new to serving can be vastly different from what we know to be true—that is why observing a class is such a great tool. Before you get all high pressure, tell them to come observe one Sunday and see if they like it. We used to do this in admissions all the time. If someone who is about to spend $100,000 on a private education wants to experience what a class is like beforehand to ease his or her fears or worries, I'm all for it.

Observing really helps the potential leader visualize serving, as well as create some interaction with current leaders so they can share their positive experiences with the prospective volunteer. It also helps a prospective volunteer get a sense of the community they will be a part of as a member of your team.

It is also a very good idea to have a thorough handbook. My current handbook is 16 pages, and it is what I spend the bulk of our time going through during an interview/orientation with a new volunteer. Everything from the code of conduct to our philosophy of how to engage kids and develop an authentic faith is part of this meeting. This way, I know each volunteer who is serving in my ministry understands our vision, our purpose, and our methods for achieving that vision right from the start.

If you don't have a handbook, spend time writing one for your ministry and make it as thorough as you know how. This also provides a great fallback in the event you have a leader who doesn't work out. I'm happy to share mine if you want a framework. Some parts of every handbook are universal for all kids or youth ministries, but some things should be unique to your flavor of ministry.

OK. You've got your handbook. You've got your process for onboarding volunteers. You know God is giving you exactly what you need…are you ready for what comes next? Of course, you are!

I wish there were some magical silver bullet or cookie-cutter approach to recruiting volunteers in every church, but each church has its own unique culture, so what works in some places may not work in others.

Parents of kids who are either almost out or already out of the ministry are great people to approach. I recommend some heavy compliments on their parenting as an opener. You don't have to lie to them, but recognizing that they have done a good job with their kids goes a long way to helping them recognize the impact they could have on other kids. Julie was a great mother who already knew me and the ministry because her son was a part of it. Those parents tend to be easy to ask, while others can be a bit nerve-racking.

One mother that God put on my heart had two sons who were EGRs (Extra Grace Required). Her older son was a natural leader, but he was always challenging the authority of my team and of me directly. It had taken a few years, but both boys had come to realize that there was nothing they could do that would change my heart for including them. After spending some time getting to know them over ice cream and cupcakes and baptizing their oldest son, their family was attending regularly, and the boys were doing well. I had always seen the time this mother had in service as a much-needed respite from two very strong-willed boys that she homeschooled during the week. I was a bit nervous about asking her and being shot down, but one day, when she picked up her son after service, I asked to talk to her. I got a heavy eye roll that had become almost a reflex over the years of issues with her boys. I could tell in her mind she was thinking, "What did the boys do now?". But when I asked her if she would pray about serving in kids ministry, she responded immediately.

"You know, I've been really praying about how to give back to the church and where to serve." It turns out that God talks to others about serving, too! We talked for a bit about how much of a commitment she could make as her husband was already serving in another ministry, and I gave her an application. When we met for the interview, she told me what she really longed for was to invest in some of the preteen girls. Being in a house with so much testosterone, she welcomed the opportunity to invest in girls that children's ministry could give her.

Many times, God is preparing someone to meet the need you have months or even years in advance, but he tends to let you do the inviting. There is a faith culmination when God puts someone on your heart to ask, and when you do, they confirm everything God told you. What I want to highlight in this story is there was a relationship, an investment I had given to that family before I asked them something. I had built relationship capital with the mom over the span of two years, and I had earned the admiration of their parents because I had taken the time to care about her boys while other churches had just kicked them out for bad behavior.

Start with families where you have already made relational investments to begin recruiting. It can be pretty challenging to recruit a complete stranger, and what if you soon realize they are not a good fit? Talk about shooting yourself in the foot! It's much more natural to talk to that couple in your small group or that parent of a sixth grader.

Also, try to limit the number of high-pressure sales pitches you give to people in the lobby on a Sunday. It will not take long for word to get out, and everyone will avoid you. If it seems like all you care about is filling a spot on your roster and not actually caring about the people you are talking with, it's pretty easy for people to shoot you down faster than a cheerleader at a chess club meeting.

When people you care about see that you have a need, there is a much stronger buy-in and much better retention of that leader. Retention is also something we will talk about in-depth in the following chapter, as it is part of a long-term strategy for volunteer success.

In review, here are the strategies that have paid off for me when it comes to recruiting:

1. Have a thorough handbook and policies that protect your ministry and your leaders.

2. Have a solid process to move a potential volunteer through (application, interview, orientation, observing a classroom, pairing with veteran leaders).

3. Ask God to direct you to certain individuals.

4. Have a "pitch" for serving that communicates why serving in your ministry matters.

5. Take advantage of church potlucks, picnics, and other events to recruit new leaders.

6. Look for under-utilized populations like students or retirees.

7. Create a conversation about overall leader development in your church and how ministries can support one another.

8. Never compromise your standards just to fill a spot.

CHAPTER
SEVEN
FINDING THE RIGHT MODEL

Have you ever heard the expression *There's more than one way to skin a cat?* This expression always confused me. Who is skinning cats? What use would I have for a cat skin? Have you ever heard someone brag, *this coat is genuine cat skin*? Or someone says, I just discovered a new way to skin a cat!?

When it comes to children's ministry, there is more than one way to skin a cat, meaning there is more than one way to teach kids about God and His Holy Word. I don't consider myself an expert on all forms of children's church because there are many I have never experienced. One thing I have to admit is that just because I haven't experienced a particular method of ministering to kids doesn't mean it isn't effective. Another thing I will admit is that just because a church is using the same models and methods now as they did forty years ago does not mean kids won't get anything out of the church. And still another thing I know to be true is just because it worked last year doesn't mean it will work again this year (thanks a lot, COVID!).

Being a creative person, I tend to get restless doing things the same way year after year. I'm always in competition with myself, trying to make what I'm doing more effective, of higher quality, and more engaging for a wider variety of people. Just because our VBS was a success and saw dozens of kids come to Jesus doesn't mean we should keep doing it that way for the next decade. I have to admire people who are able to do the same thing week in and week out. Society would be doomed if people like me worked in factories or accounting firms, always trying to change things—but I'm not working there.

I had an amazing volunteer who had been working in the same chicken plant for over 30 years. Every day, that plant processed thousands of chickens. One day, I asked her how things had changed over 30 years of doing the same job, and I was surprised to learn there had been marked improvements to the process that made her job easier. The company has got new machines that make the butchering process cleaner and more efficient. There was new software to help with shipping. New government regulations had to be observed. All of this resulted in an end product that was essentially the same as it was in 1990, but the methods had been improved while efficiency increased. This company had found its model for producing chicken, and for the most part, the end result stayed the same because customers weren't clamoring for a new and improved chicken tender. The *model* was found, and once it worked, it didn't need to be changed, although the *method* was in an almost constant state of flux.

Having known my wife for 20 years, I'd like to think I know her better than anyone else in the world. For instance, I know that encouragement goes way further than criticism. I know that she can learn anything and that her primary motivation for everything she does is to help other people. My experience and knowledge of her strengths and weaknesses inform what responsibilities I let her run with and which responsibilities I try to take off her plate because they will frustrate or exhaust her.

Many times, when I look at the model of how a ministry is running, be it a large group/small group model, a classroom model, or something else, I see many church leaders who are frustrated or exhausted. To use yet another sports analogy, they are trying to play football with a basketball team.

What do I mean by that?

Basketball and football require vastly different approaches to be successful. A football team is actually a team made up of 3 distinct teams, each with a different role: offense, defense, and special teams. Within each team, there are specialized players that have a specialized role, like a defensive back, a safety, an offensive lineman, a quarterback, or a kicker. Each one has a different set of skills and even a different body type suited for their position. Each of those sub-teams has its own coach or coordinator who works to improve its players in each of their specialized roles.

You could compare this to a children's ministry with nursery, pre-k, and elementary teams. Each team is going to work in a very different way and will need different training. My nursery volunteers are going to need very different skills than an elementary small group leader.

This model works really well when you have a robust team with skilled leaders. But perhaps you're feeling frustrated every week because you're trying to develop football players when what God has given you this season is actually a basketball team.

A basketball player is expected to be good both on offense and defense. While there are different positions in basketball, every player has to be flexible enough to fit in different plays depending on the team they are competing against. So, instead of having a specialized volunteer who works exclusively with 3rd-grade girls, you may need to train them to be prepared for a few different environments so you can use that volunteer in a pre-k room or in front of the elementary class. If I were given a choice, I'd take a volunteer who is adaptable to serving in a few different places over a superstar leader who only feels called to one specific role or one specific age group.

As the leader of the ministry, you can set this expectation during your recruitment process. I have some volunteers who tell me they only want to hold babies, or they won't change diapers, or are afraid of how pre-teen boys smell, and want to serve in a specific "football-model" role. Setting the expectation that you will try to get them into their preferred area, but there may be Sundays when we need them to help with another age group, can go a long way in balancing their expectations with the reality of the ministry. It might just open their eyes, too.

Different churches have different expectations for their volunteers. Some with multiple services may expect their volunteers in kids or youth ministries to attend one service and serve another. Other churches with one service may ask volunteers to serve once or twice a month.

Leaders might serve for a semester, or they may be expected to serve until Jesus comes what you have to decide as the leader of the ministry is how to balance keeping leaders connected with kids and avoiding burning out your leaders.

When leaders are scarce, it is very hard to allow any of them to take a Sunday off—especially if you have to close rooms as a result. You may need to run this situation by your church leadership and get final approval from them. Is it more important that spots are filled and rooms stay open or that your leaders also get to attend church services regularly? Maybe you need to define what "regular church service attendance" looks like at your church. This is an important distinction for you and your volunteers.

When I was hired as the Children's Pastor at a church in Georgia, my senior pastor talked about how much he wanted me to be able to attend service regularly. Being able to actually participate in worship is one of the biggest sacrifices children's pastors make in their role. If someone calls out sick, there are more kids than expected, or a kid busts their lip during a game, I can kiss the attending service goodbye. Months would go by when I was not able to attend service for one reason or another.

One Sunday, our kindergarten teacher for the first service was out sick. We had a handful of kindergarteners, so I had them join the rest of the elementary students in the main kids' room. I then proceeded to go to service with my wife. The next day, that same senior pastor—who had reassured me so many times of the importance of attending service while I was interviewing for the position— asked me why we had closed the kindergarten room. I replied that our teacher was sick, and we combined the kids with another classroom. "But you were in service. You could have taught that class and not closed it," he insisted.

And the penny drops.

At that moment, I understood a very unsettling reality: my attendance in church was not as important to the leaders in the church as it was for our children's ministry to look healthy and all our rooms to be open. Needless to say, my church attendance got even less frequent in the next year as I felt I had to handle any potential room closure, emergency, or craft supply issue myself, lest my senior pastor feel like I wasn't doing my job.

I know I am not alone in this feeling. Maybe you are close to burning out because you can't even remember the last time you went to service and were able to receive with the reckless abandon what other members of your congregation do. It can be very isolating to feel like you are not part of the adult community in your own church simply because of your responsibilities in that church. And yet, so many Children's pastors across so many denominations face this dilemma. It can feel very isolating when you are sitting at a staff meeting, and everyone else talks about what happened during the service on Sunday, and you have no idea because you were doing your job in another part of the building.

Taking the opportunity to have an honest conversation with your church leadership about the realities of your position and their expectations of how your ministry should function can go a long way in giving you the freedom to tinker with your method of doing ministry. It may just enable a healthier balance between ministering and receiving.

All I know is that if your method for ministry requires you to be in the trenches every service every week, it will drain your passion for ministry.

CHAPTER EIGHT

PASTOR & DIRECTOR BURNOUT

One of the greatest challenges related to serving in kid's ministry is that it requires volunteers and leaders to miss church services. If you happen to serve in a church with multiple services, this isn't as big of an issue as those who have one Sunday service. While you may have the best of intentions to attend service regularly, most children's ministry leaders are one call-out, no-show, or discipline problem away from missing service on any given Sunday. Couple this with the reality that many children's pastors and directors feel disconnected from their church staff and church congregations, and it's easy to see why the turnover rate in children's and youth ministry is so high.

I took another informal Facebook survey among Children's pastors and asked them how often they get to attend a FULL service. There is a big distinction between sliding in the back row for most of the sermon and attending a full service.

The good news is that 40% of children's pastors have balanced their ministerial responsibilities in such a way that allows them to attend services every week. The bad news is that more than 1/3 of the directors and pastors I surveyed attend *less than once a quarter—if at all.* Reasons for this troubling attendance trend vary; some (like me) get to participate in worship and then oversee the children's transition from service to the kid's area, some don't have enough leaders to step away, or some might just dislike their pastor's preaching and don't have the heart to tell him.

HOW OFTEN DO YOU ATTEND A FULL WORSHIP SERVICE?

180 | EVERY WEEK

114 LESS THAN ONCE EVERY 3 MONTHS

105 | NEVER

72 | ONCE A MONTH

67 EVERY 2-3 WEEKS

60 ONCE EVERY FEW MONTHS

What this survey did show is that for a majority of Children's Pastors, service attendance among staff is not the highest priority for their church's leadership. There's a bit of irony here because I always hear lead pastors talk about the importance of meeting together. I hear those same pastors lament about people watching online instead of showing up in person because being a part of the body of Christ means being together and interacting. Yet, those same pastors don't have the same passion to ensure that all of the staff get to receive from a worship service. It's an endemic problem that highlights where the true priorities of churches lie, and it's not in leaders participating in worship. Ask your worship or media leaders when they last got to just attend a service without any responsibilities. (I bet their numbers would be even more lopsided.)

At my previous church, I felt alone in my ministry role compared to the other staff. The children's area was in the basement of our building, so rather unintentionally, the design of the building created a disconnect between the kids' ministry and the church at large. We were running our own programs, had our own media team, had our own policies and procedures, and many adults without children had never been in our space or even knew it existed. During staff meetings, everyone else would talk about something that happened during service, and I never knew what they were talking about because I had not been able to attend the main service.I did my best to listen to the podcast of the sermon later in the week. I did my best to keep my own spiritual life strong, and we did have a small group we were a part of. Yet, in so many ways, I was starving. Starving for community. Starving for validation from church leadership to tell me that what I was doing actually mattered. Starving to feel like I belonged to our church and not just my ministry.

How long can someone feel this way before burnout takes hold?

Chances are good that you are experiencing burnout in some form as you read this book. Nothing crushes the spirit faster than someone who puts their heart and soul into a lesson, only for kids to respond with blank stares or fart noises. Nothing can make you want to quit faster than getting complaints from parents who themselves refuse to serve yet expect their kids to be entertained, educated, and engaged whenever they see fit to drop them off.

So, how are Children's Pastors and Directors supposed to stay healthy in this environment where we are continually understaffed, under-appreciated, and spiritually underfed?

I wish I had a silver bullet for this problem. I wish I had a fool-proof method for making sure you are spiritually fed and part of the community in which you serve in such an important role. I'm sure most senior pastors wish I did, too.

Part of the solution is making sure you have a healthy, fully-staffed ministry with leaders you can trust to run things while you step away. *(But Brian! I never have a fully staffed ministry! Someone is always calling out or quitting. I can never catch up! If that were the case, I wouldn't be reading this book!!!!)*

When I say fully staffed, I don't always mean there are no holes. Remember, as I said at the beginning, God gives you everything you need to do the ministry he wants you to do. Ergo, you have all the leaders necessary for your ministry to survive one service without you. If you don't, then you may need to suggest the idea that the children's ministry is closed 2-4 Sundays a year to give your team a respite. Many churches use 5th Sundays for this purpose and make those Sundays a family service, giving kids ministry a week off. Right now, my church is shuttering down children's ministry on major holiday weekends, where we typically have very light attendance.

If you, as a leader, want to be effective, you have to find a way to prevent burnout in your own spiritual life before anything else. Maybe you can find a church with a Saturday night or Sunday night service that you can go to and just receive. Maybe you can create a Bible study with some other leaders that meet regularly. If you are feeling isolated from the rest of your staff or church, the best thing to do is talk to your elders or senior pastor about it. Most senior pastors want you to be at your best and be getting fed, but I've also found that throwing a problem in your senior pastor's lap is not a recipe for things changing. When telling your leadership that you are feeling burnt out or isolated, also come up with some ideas of how that could change. Tell them what would recharge your spirit. For me, having a day of solitude and prayer where I can go off by myself and connect with God is far more recharging than sitting at a Kid's ministry conference for 3 days. Finding two or three other pastors from other churches to meet with regularly will help me feel connected far more than listening to sermon podcasts.

In many ways, Senior Pastors are in the same boat as they rarely get to receive from the sermon they are preaching. Coming up with a way for you to attend service even once a month will go a long way to help you feel like you are part of the church and not just serving the church.

One of the best ways to guard against burning yourself out is to train others to handle your responsibilities. I didn't really come to terms with this issue until we were close to having our 4th child. I had been at my Georgia church for a few years and had strong leaders in almost all key positions—most of whom were there during the interim period before I was hired. So, I knew when I took paternity leave, they could handle it. But the problem was in those few years, I had put in a few new systems, like a new check-in system, media software for our large groups, and a few other things that I had learned the ins and outs of but had not really trained anyone else how to manage. I had half a dozen leaders who worked the check-in stations, but none of them knew how to change our check-in stations from the mid-week event to the Sunday service event. No one else knew what to do when the printer wasn't recognized by the iPads. I had plenty of leaders who could prepare a lesson, but not one who knew how to download the curriculum from the website and what folder it went in. I had a team of worship motion dancers, but no one knew what channel the wireless mic got plugged into or how to get our computer to recognize the projector.

Can I just ask—why is it so hard for laptops to recognize projectors? I mean, it should be really easy. You should just plug it in, and bam! Dual screens. But it never seems to be that simple. You have to do it 6 times and fail and then do it the same way again, but on the 7th try, it decides to work. Not only that but what's with screen resolution? It's 2024, and we can't agree on a universal resolution for all screens. Cars can drive themselves now. I can find the weather report in Alaska by just asking my phone, but a laptop and a projector can't have the same resolution. End rant.

There is a difference between users and administrators in any software you utilize. Users know how to operate something as long as everything is functioning properly. Administrators have to know how to solve problems to get something **back to** functioning properly. And do these problems happen on Tuesday afternoon? Of course not! They happen on Sunday morning with a room full of rambunctious kids.

When I was a media pastor, I experienced this often. It's easy to have a volunteer sit down at the computer with ProPresenter up and running, all the files organized correctly and ready to run by just pressing the spacebar (user). It's a whole other challenge to call a volunteer and say, "I'm sick. Can you put the service together in ProPresenter before Sunday?" That requires knowledge of where the files are, how to build new lyrics, how to import Bible verses, setting up second monitor displays, creating slides from the pastor's notes that were supposed to be sent on Thursday but didn't get emailed until Saturday afternoon, etc. (admin).

Do you see the difference in what someone has to know?

All administrators start out as users; that is how they get comfortable learning. But if you don't move people into admin roles by training them in the boring and idiosyncratic minutia of the systems, you will constantly find yourself doing all that work when things go awry. Some paid leaders might argue that all the admin stuff is their job, but I would say this is untrue. Your job is not managing volunteer scheduling apps, putting all the lesson videos on thumb drives, and setting up the sound system in the kid's area for the next 10 years. The calling you accepted was to build up and invest in leaders and equip them to do these tasks so that you can be freed up to do other things—like actually making relationships with kids and parents. You know, the fun and meaningful stuff.

If all your volunteers are *users* and you are not training or empowering some of them to be *administrators* for these systems, you will burn yourself out.

One of my solutions heading into paternity leave was creating what I called **The Book of Brian.** This book was sort of a worst-case scenario manual in the event I got hit by a bus. As I thought through what needed to be in it, I realized that it needed to answer any question I could see coming up if I suddenly wasn't there. It also needed to be easy to read and understand.

Luckily, I knew I had a few months before we had our baby, so I had time to make a thorough, visual guide for everything from check-in setup to scheduling volunteers to downloading and importing curriculum. My goal was to create a clear and concise how-to book that any leader could read and be able to become an administrator.

Through my years in ministry, I have encountered certain insecure leaders who are deathly afraid of creating something like this because they are worried that once volunteers know how to do their jobs, there won't be any use for them anymore. Such a worry is short-sided and will ultimately stunt your ministry. You are limiting both the growth potential of your volunteers and how much your ministry can grow because it will ultimately bump up against your maximum bandwidth.

Pastors who don't equip their teams with the tools to do their jobs in their absence aren't creating job security for themselves— they are creating volunteers who will grow tired of never being entrusted with more and quit. This leads to another area of burnout that goes hand in hand with Leader burnout: Volunteer burnout.

CHAPTER NINE

VOLUNTEER BURNOUT

As I said before, burned-out leadership goes hand in hand with burned-out volunteers. If you are burning out, you have to fix some of the big issues before starting to address the issues facing your team.

One of the best ways to keep volunteers is to have a ministry that is organized and well-run. That comes from the top down. If you consistently recruit leaders who quit soon after starting in kids ministry, that may be a sign that something in your ministry needs more of your attention. It could be that you have a volunteer that is hard for others to work with, or the atmosphere of your ministry is cold to newcomers. This is part of why I make sure I know my core leaders well, can trust them to be inclusive, and also not scare off new leaders by being bossy, territorial, or rude. If you see some of these attributes come through with your established leaders, it may be good to have a meeting where you help them see the value in newly recruited leaders having a positive experience right away in your ministry. It may mean having tough conversations with veteran leaders about their attitudes. When veteran leaders complain that they wish they had more help, it's pretty easy to take that moment to help them see the value in getting a new volunteer to stay long-term.

Think about how much companies spend to get you as a customer. If it's for something like cable, a cell phone, or a gym, that company has an entire department devoted to keeping you as a customer and not losing your business. They might give you a discount for a while, send a technician to address quality issues, show you how to use the free weights—whatever it takes to keep you. That's because the company knows how much it took to get you as a customer in the first place, and keeping their current customers happy is much cheaper and easier than trying to get new customers. They might not keep 100% of people that want to cancel, but they will try everything they can before simply letting you cancel.

If a volunteer emails you (it's rarely face-to-face) and says they can't serve anymore, find out why. What's causing them to want to quit? It may be something you can change, or it may be something that's out of your hands—but at the very least, have the conversation. Ask the questions that will clue you into the culture of your ministry and the volunteers they served with.

Another thing I learned while working in college admissions was to plan for attrition. Inevitably, no matter how excited students were to register for classes, around 20-30% would drop out after a week or not even show up at all. New volunteers in kids ministry or youth ministry can be the same way. You may meet with someone who sounds excited and passionate, only to have them flake after serving once or twice. Having leaders quit is impossible to avoid—it will happen, and it's not always your fault. Many of them will feel a tremendous amount of guilt and may avoid you. All you can do is try to follow up with them. Let every volunteer know that working with youth or kids isn't for everyone, and it's ok if this ministry is not for them. If that's the case, connect them with another ministry leader that can guide that person to a position that is better suited to their skills or strengths. Your goal with this population is to try your best to understand why they quit and do what you can to remedy that. What you have to do is let them know you are not mad at them.

Many volunteers who quit feel like they let you or even all the kids in your church down. If you can find a way to end their time in kids ministry on a positive note, it will help the reputation of your ministry in the church. What you don't want is for one new leader's bad experience serving in your ministry to be shared with everyone they know in the church.

WHAT ARE YOU DOING TO HELP YOUR VOLUNTEER FEEL LIKE THEIR EFFORTS MATTER?

It's amazing to me how many leaders work so hard to recruit volunteers only to throw them into a chaotically run ministry, then wonder why that volunteer doesn't last. If volunteers walk into a ministry role where, for starters, they don't have any buy-in, they have no way to communicate ideas or concerns, and the volunteer isn't honored for their sacrifice, that is a recipe for burnout among the volunteers in your ministry.

A major event that can kill your momentum in growing your leader roster is when you lose leaders who have served for a long time. I had one leader who had served in our kid's ministry for over 10 years and decided to step down when our church reopened after COVID.

"I didn't realize how nice it was to just be able to go to church and not worry about teaching. Once I had a few months to rest, I realized just how burnt out I was," she confessed to me.

Burnout is a tough concept because it can mean different things to different people. What causes one person to burn out might be an easy burden for another to carry. Some leaders serve 48-50 Sundays a year seemingly without complaint, while others serve for a month and then quit because they have "too much going on." Burnout among longtime volunteers is another area that requires you to look critically at what you are expecting out of your leaders.

Are you asking too much of them? Are you expecting too little? Are they feeling isolated and trapped in their room with little input or buy-in? Are they scrambling every Sunday to get the lesson ready because copies weren't made or the video wasn't playing correctly? Is there a difficult child in their class that they lack the skills to deal with? Taking inventory in these areas will help you see the ministry through their eyes, and addressing these concerns can bring honor to the task of teaching and engaging kids in your church. The real question is: What are *you* doing to help your volunteers feel like their efforts matter?

If you've been in Christian circles for any length of time, you've probably heard of Gary Chapman's 5 Love Languages. (At last count, I think there are about 978 variations of this book.) When it comes to honoring your volunteers, you have to speak their love language in order to encourage them. I don't come out and ask them their love language in my application, but I do have a few systems that tend to hit most of the love languages throughout the year.

The first is thank you cards. If you have a ministry team of 10-20 people, there is no reason why each volunteer shouldn't get between 3-4 cards from you a year. Maybe you make sure to send them a birthday card (Confession time: I'm not as good at this as I should be). If I have a volunteer who really knocked something out of the park, like a role in VBS, teaching a great lesson, or having to clean up some kid's puke, etc, make sure to send them a hand-written card. Just a few sentences that acknowledge their work and remind them that what they are doing matters. How often do you get that from your employer or family member? Not very often. Getting a deliberate form of acknowledgment goes a long way.

The second is small gifts. Two questions I do ask in my application are the volunteer's favorite candy and favorite restaurant. If they do something stellar, I might couple that thank you card with their favorite candy or a gift card to a restaurant they like. Knowing what they like is helpful in making a gift feel thoughtful. I can't tell you how many Starbucks cards I've gotten over the years from well-intentioned people who are unaware that I don't drink coffee. I still find a way to use it, and it's still a nice

Maria,

Thank you for jumping in with our preschool class and calming Sarah down on Sunday.

You are making a huge difference in the lives of these kids.

In Christ,
Pastor Brian

thought, but if they really know me, they'll get me a gift card to the LEGO store. That small bit of knowledge helps a gift become thoughtful instead of generic.

The third is team parties. It's fairly easy to schedule a Christmas party for your team. I make sure I allocate some budget so that I can afford to get them all $5-10 gifts around Christmas time. Once, we had a party on January 3rd because of the Christmas program. Whenever it happens, I invite everyone on my team over to my house, have some great food, play some fun games, and give them gifts. Who is going to complain about that? I also try to do a volunteer appreciation event once a year-usually after Easter or in May. This might be something you do church-wide for all your volunteers, but if your church doesn't do it for everyone, at the very least, do it for your team. Remember, these are the elite volunteers in the church. Their sacrifice is worth honoring them with a dinner and a little pageantry a few times a year.

So, just in these three ways, I've hit Words of Encouragement, Gifts, Quality Time, and the Acts of Service Love Languages. (I would strongly recommend you don't try to show physical touch. Hopefully, you already know not to touch your volunteers, but if you didn't before, you do now.) These also go a long way to increasing morale. Much like a sports team, being aware of your team's morale is crucial to keeping them serving long-term. Griping and complaining from your volunteers can be a sign of low morale. Not having supplies or necessary materials can also take a toll on morale.

When I started at the church in Georgia, morale was low. Leaders had been holding the ministry together for over a year without any leadership. Our senior pastor did not visit the kid's area or make an effort to connect with the leaders consistently, so they felt isolated and taken for granted. Not only that, but the ministry had been underfunded, and the facilities in the kid's area had not been maintained well. When I arrived, I was astonished to discover that over half of all the lightbulbs in all the kid's rooms were burnt out or not working entirely. It was dark and had a creepy haunted hospital vibe. Definitely not the first impression I wanted to make on new families.

In my second week, I spent $150 on lightbulbs and lamps for all the rooms. When my volunteers came in that Sunday, they said, "It looks so bright in here! We have been waiting for these lights to get fixed for months!" As it turns out, because they felt isolated and disconnected from the leadership in the church, the kid's team didn't have a point of contact on staff to go to for simple needs like light bulbs or supplies. The crayons were all broken, the markers were dried out, and the Play-Doh was all mixed together. How do you think that environment impacted morale? Coming in every week, trying to make do with poor lighting and inadequate supplies, doesn't exactly scream "you matter" to the volunteers that were serving. What's worse is there was a low-level resentment brewing toward the senior pastor as they saw the church make investments in other ministries and neglect kids ministry.

To be clear, the senior pastor was spending time and resources to find a Children's Pastor, but the volunteers could not see that on Sundays. The only thing the volunteers experienced was a feeling of abandonment during that period of time.

Low morale and burnout are often tied to the same root issues. Finding ways to identify what's wrong, fixing it, and finding ways to create the best environment possible for your team to serve will go a long way in increasing the longevity of your volunteers. And the more volunteers you can keep long term, the less recruiting you will have to do, and the stronger and more experienced your team will be.

Let's look at some of these root issues that lead to volunteer burnout?

1. Failure to Cast Vision When Making Changes

As you lead a team, it is critical for you, the leader, to cast a vision for any changes you want to make. Gathering your team and pronouncing a new system, process, or expectation without first helping them understand why it's happening can leave your volunteers confused and even resentful. And it doesn't take very long for that resentment to become a source of burnout for your team. Let me give you an example:

For those of you who have had kids attending grade school from about 2010 on, you may have noticed one subject is very different than it was when we were kids: math.

Now, I'm not sure why we needed to change math in America. Last I checked, we were all able to add, multiply, divide, and even subtract using the old tried-and-true methods we were taught in the 20th century, getting the right answer every time. I never walk into a store, see a 25% off, and think to myself, "I wish they would invent a new way of doing math so I can figure out how much money I'm going to save on these shoes."

To the best of my knowledge, there was no nationwide push by parents to create a new, completely foreign process of adding 37 and 18 that now takes an entire sheet of paper.

Maybe other countries were laughing at our math skills behind our backs. Maybe the Dutch were making fun of how Americans add and subtract. Regardless, my kids and your kids are being taught *Common Core Math*, and it is so completely different than the old math. I know that it makes me frustrated when I'm trying to help my kids with homework.

No education board would make this giant overhaul to such a basic and essential subject in school if they didn't believe it was better. I would hope that school boards were given the data and research and found Common Core to be superior to the math skills currently being taught in schools across the country. Someone somewhere had to see the benefit of teaching Common Core math and had to win over an influential group of educators to the idea of completely changing math. The problem is that influential groups never cast a vision to all those parents who would not be able to understand the math of the new generation. If someone could plainly and passionately explain why Common Core math is going to help my kids be better at math in a way I understand, then I would cease being a critic and become a champion of this amazing new way of doing things. Instead of educators casting a vision on why we needed to change math, it just kind of happened. One day, my daughter brings home a math problem with all this extra stuff that I don't understand.

Do your volunteers feel like they are now expected to understand Common Core math? When you make a change that seems totally reasonable and necessary to your ministry, does your team understand why it was done and how this new change will benefit them in their role of helping kids? Did you give anyone on your team a chance to speak about the decision or into the process before you made it? Let's use a practical example:

In Youth and Children's Ministries, safety has to always be the #1 priority. The environment your teens and kids are in has to be a safe environment, physically, emotionally, spiritually, and relationally. I believe one of the best ways to guard that safety is by having video cameras in each room. To me, cameras provide obvious positive benefits for leaders, parents, and the church itself, but others could see cameras as an invasion of privacy or evidence of a lack of trust. Were I to simply put cameras in the rooms with no explanation, I'm allowing each person's own interpretation of my actions to run rampant. While my intentions were to protect the leaders and our ministry, it could be taken as an offense, and that offense could grow into resentment.

Instead, before I have the camera installed, I need to become a camera evangelist. I need to share the good news about cameras and why we want to put them in with all my leaders. I need to shape the narrative of what is going on so they see the change as a benefit to them and not a lack of trust. If I say, "We're thinking of putting cameras in the rooms, how do you feel about that?" I'm giving my leaders a chance to be heard, and I'm also able to speak to their feedback.

If I had a leader, say, "I don't like the idea of someone watching everything I'm doing." I can address that concern:

"We are putting cameras in because we want to protect you, not to spy on you. Imagine if a parent calls me irate, saying something happened to their kid in your class. Wouldn't it be nice to have a way to go back and see exactly what happened to show that parent? I trust you, and I know that you are amazing with those kids. I just want to make sure a simple misunderstanding doesn't blow up into something that sours your experience serving our families experience in attending. Cameras can help us with that."

2. My Way or the Highway

As a volunteer, I served under many different kinds of leaders. Some leaders were humble, some were arrogant, some were indecisive, some were jerks, some were fantastic role models and some seemed to be on a power trip. Serving under a leader who squashes debate or input from their team can be a very souring experience. As a creative person with lots of ideas, it was very hard for me to serve under someone who didn't welcome or value the input and the perspectives of others. I experienced most of this dynamic as a drummer on the worship team. I learned that there are worship leaders who are comfortable letting the drummer bring their own style or sound into a song, and there are those who rip the sticks out of my hands if I deviate from the part they provided me.

As a leader, sometimes you just have to put your foot down, and many times, you need to be decisive. There are many books about this area of leadership and how to do it well. When you expect volunteers to do something "just because I say so," you are going to scare off talented people and keep people who begin to rely on you telling them *exactly* what to do and how to do it. In many cases, this type of volunteer management stems from insecurity or—at the very least—a lack of relationship capital with the members of your team.

It is important to remember that you are not the boss of your volunteers. You don't have the leverage of saying, "I'm paying you to do it, so do it and do it now!" The pastor/volunteer dynamic is so different from an employer/employee relationship because you have to find ways to motivate other than a paycheck. And even though an employee can quit at any time, the assumption is that the salary offsets some of the inconveniences and frustrations that an employee will encounter. Not so with volunteers! The only thing that truly keeps a volunteer serving is their relationships with those they serve and those they serve under.

If you, as the leader, are hoping to push your team toward some objective, you can only push so far using your title alone. There are people who still do what the pastor says because he or she is the pastor, but that pool of people is very small. Answering the why question for your team will go a long way toward building trust and creating a team that supports your vision.

3. Being indecisive

Imagine if you were on a football team (for me, that's a stretch because I was not built for football). You and your teammates practice running plays, learn your routes, and work on all the fundamentals that help you score touchdowns and win games. Your team has suited up and comes out of the locker room fired up to play and win. You get the ball and start working your way down the field, but once you get to your opponent's 20-yard line, the location of the end zone suddenly changes to the opposite end of the field without warning. Now, you have to turn around and work your way back down the field. As you begin toward your new end zone, a referee calls a penalty for too many men on the field. The rules have just changed, and instead of playing with 11 men, you now have to play with nine, and you can no longer throw the ball; you can only run with the ball. Then, once you get to the 20-yard line with the end zone in view, its location changes again—this time outside the stadium in the parking lot. How long until your team walks off in frustration, refusing to keep playing?

In order to keep volunteers committed and filled with purpose, your objective must be laser-focused. You have to know where you want to go and what you want to do, and making any adjustments to that goal must be done very carefully. That's why, in most professional sports, changes to the rules are typically made the year BEFORE the start of a new season. Why? Because changing how the game is played has major implications for every team. Imagine the chaos it would cause to a sport if rules were modified every week or even every month.

Your volunteers need stability, and they need to understand why they serve. If you keep changing how they are serving and where they are serving, they will soon question *why* they are serving. It is interesting that Jesus himself referred to congregations as a flock of sheep. Some might hear that analogy and be offended by it, like Jesus thinks we are mindless followers who just do what we're told, but I see it differently. All people crave leadership and relationships. Some people want to be in charge, but God designed us in such a way that not everybody wants the responsibilities and stress that come with leadership. Some people just want to be part of something great, but they are looking for someone else to cast the vision for what is great.

If their leader keeps changing their mind, changing their methods, and changing their vision, it can lead to chaos, and most people don't like chaos.

This is why things like curriculum and having a handbook for your team are so important: they provide stability and a rhythm that allows your team to know what to expect. If a leader keeps changing their mind or avoids making tough decisions, chaos follows, and volunteers stop following.

4. Not listening to your team

I don't know anyone who loves being ignored. I also don't know anyone who likes to be in a conversation with someone who is obviously not listening. You may have way more knowledge and even more experience than the members of your team, or their ideas may be absolutely terrible, but there is always a way to make someone feel heard when they talk to you.

When it's time for us to start planning VBS, our creative team will have plenty of meetings where we try to hone in on what we are doing and how it will all get done. I always come into these meetings with a fairly clear idea of what I want, and I've given thought to how I want to do it, but I always leave space for people's input. I want to make sure that everyone who is putting their shoulder to the spiritual plow of a church event is able to share their ideas with the group and feel like their idea was considered and they were heard. For most people, that's enough validation and respect. There will always be some who can be a bit more arrogant and want to use this opportunity to show everyone how creative or skilled they are. If you have dealt with a personality like this on your team, it might make you cautious to ask for feedback or ideas because a strong personality can quickly take your meeting off the rails.

It doesn't have to be every meeting or every bible lesson, but giving your volunteers a place to voice their ideas and concerns will help everyone have ownership and share in the vision of the ministry. Give your volunteers a seat at the table. Don't make the mistake of being a dictator because you will scare off talented volunteers who want to do more than whatever you tell them to do.

CONCLUSION

While all these observations and ideas are not foolproof, implementing some of them should help you tackle one of the biggest struggles in ministry. Placing your hopes in one day having "enough" volunteers instead of using what you have will continue to prove frustrating.

The only way to truly have the right amount of leaders, the right budget, or the right space is to see it through God's eyes. God has given you exactly what you need in this ministry! You have to believe that, or you will constantly find yourself stressed out, overwhelmed, and butting your head against a wall. While one church's budget and resources may look entirely different from another, coveting what that other church has or trying to copy it in your setting is a recipe for burnout.

It may seem overly simplistic to tell you to be content, like a dad pulling you past a toy store while you whine to go inside, but it is the perspective through which God has lifted the burdens and stress off my shoulders. Living in the knowledge that God meets all your needs frees you from having to make it all happen on your own.

Remember, you are not alone when you feel like you are short on volunteers. In fact, you are in good company if it feels like your ministry needs more help. Over 50% of leaders in children's and youth ministries say they need leaders more than anything else.

While I hope you're encouraged knowing everyone wants more volunteers, I really hope you understand that the only way to stay sane is to learn how to use the resources you have instead of hoping and praying for more year after year. When it comes to resources, also look at any resources you do have at your disposal and figure out how to leverage them—whether it's young, eager teens who are willing to help or leaders you could promote from other ministry areas into your elite volunteer team of kids and youth.

Take some time to think through your process of onboarding new volunteers. Put yourself in the shoes of someone who may be intimidated by the idea of working with kids. The clearer your system, the more comfortable new volunteers will feel in your ministry. Remember that overwhelming new volunteers leads to attrition, and those overwhelmed former volunteers will share their experience with others, making it even harder to recruit.

If your ministry is going to have a reputation among the members of your church, let it be for excellence! Create an environment where people want to serve or are even excited to serve! This can only happen if your ministry is organized and the volunteers feel supported and heard.

Hopefully, you are coming away with both helpful tools to recruit, onboard, and retain volunteers, but more importantly, I hope you are coming away with a new perspective on how to operate your ministry, free from the influence of ministry models that are not tailored to your church's specific needs and resources.

Your ministry colleagues and your volunteers don't want to see you quit the ministry and start selling used cars and neither do I. My hope is that this little book has given you some encouragement and hopefully, a path through the dark forest of ministry discouragement.

God has you in this ministry for a reason, and the devil would love nothing more than to bog you down with feelings of irrelevance, discouragement and hopelessness. If there is one thing I have seen in our culture, it's that the next generation is under attack. Kids and teens are struggling with situations and circumstances that are completely foreign to the adults in their lives. What kids and teens need more than anything is Godly examples that remain in their lives as the grow into adults.

In the 70s and 80s, we saw an all-out spiritual attack on marriages that continued into the twenty-first century. Now, there's less than a 50% chance the kids in your ministry are living in a home with both their parents. While many kids are dealing with the reality of an unstable home, you and your volunteers can be a place of consistency and spiritual discipleship—but this can't happen if their leaders become burned out and end up quitting.

We can strengthen these ministries in ways that truly impact kids and teens because kids want to be invested in and investment takes time and energy. When we are overseeing a ministry that creates a revolving door of leaders that start serving then quit serving shortly thereafter, kids will grow apathetic.

I didn't write this book simply because youth leaders and kid's ministry leaders need help with volunteers, I wrote it because the volunteer problem has a direct connection to a lack of relationships with a population that desperately needs more positive, Godly relationships.

In 1 Corinthians 4, Paul writes that "God is not the author of confusion but of peace." Our kids and teens are living in a culture that is in a state of constant confusion. Our society has become a rudderless ship, tossed about by political, social, environmental and religious divisiveness. Acceptance and tolerance of each person's individual definition of truth and love make it nearly impossible to live out the life God has in store for our kids. Volunteers have the sacred opportunity to speak into the lives of our kids and building a valuable, impactful relationship that can help them navigate the lies and noise that saturate their formative years.

The stakes are high. The enemy is well-equipped with a variety of weapons to take you and your volunteers out of the fight. Will we trust in God's peace when that volunteer calls out sick on Sunday morning? Will you believe that God has given you everything you need to do the Ministry He has called you to do? Will you continue in ministry even if the challenges seem insurmountable right now by praying for God to reveal the method that brings peace instead of confusion?

No church is perfect. No ministry position is without its challenges, but seeing the big picture helps me look past the issues that could mutate into resentment and bitterness and ultimately disillusion with my ministry career. Realizing that God has not tasked me to do this job alone, but has brought the right people into my life and into our church community that can share the load brings me hope.

www.ingramcontent.com/pod-product-compliance
Lightning Source LLC
Chambersburg PA
CBHW072239290326
41934CB00008BB/1349